Women's Worth, Priceless

Written by a Man, for Women
Empowerment . . .

TROY MCKENZIE

Herein, I encourage the recognition of those dignified and noble women who have proved incorrect the beliefs of male chauvinism. These pioneering women have exemplified that their gender is no less able than men in the fields of academics, invention, nursing, mathematics, science, medicine, computing, and government. It shows that the priceless contributions of women to our modern world should be rightfully revered and appreciated more.

Those lofty contributions of women should serve as a source of gratification and inspiration; especially to girls to become women in those professional fields that their foremothers have been traditionally restricted and underrepresented. This is an encouragement for young women to take full advantage of the rights and prospects that their forebears have, through their tireless feminism struggles, gained for them. This is also an appeal to the conscience of the modern world to take issue with violations and deprivations of human rights. These unprincipled acts only resulted in subhuman treatments of millions of women and girls. It is an imperative of the present generation to strive for the eradication of gender discrimination in order that hundreds of millions more females of future generations may be born and live and die free from gender-based biases, violence, abuses, and inequalities.

Women's Worth: Priceless urges all nations and people to heed the call for gender equality and women's empowerment. It is only proper for all people, as worthy examples of being civilised, to hold the best interests of all members of the human family at heart. To know of injustice and inequality without meaningful opposition is an act beneath the dignity of people of goodwill. No one should be discriminated against. It must be recognised and accepted that we can make this world a utopia. In point of fact, equality provides the strongest foundation for promoting amity and peaceful coexistence between all people, without any regards whatsoever.

Acknowledgements

The author gratefully acknowledges the non-exclusive permission given by UNICEF to use excerpts from *The State of the World's Children 2007* and *The State of the World's Children 2012*.

It is acknowledged that much has changed in the decades of the advocacy of women's rights and child well-being. But even *The State of the World's Children 2014* in numbers shows that the basic idea has not, in particular children's situations.

The reports provide unabated global and national statistics of the most vulnerable women's and children's circumstances. The years these reports are published are not so significant. What matters most are the facts on which they're based; it is crucial to take action for the improvement of the lives of women and children—and imperative to realizing their rights and well-being.

consequences to keep on repeating. Disregard and contempt for women's rights only result in the evil acts of violence, inequalities, and licentiousness against millions of women and girls.

Much has been done to accelerate progress towards gender equality and empowering women through education and legislation. The waves of feminism have brought about many changes in the experience of women the world over. But more still remains to be done for the full advancement of women's human rights and fundamental freedoms. Widespread apathy among humans is an obstacle to be overcome in order to achieve greater progress and a more just world. Selfishness limits the individuals of low morals to think of their own interest. People of the sort are never eager to help solve the problems of others, only their own. But people who are guided be a moral sense of altruism know and accept that besides their own interests and problems, there are those of others. And moreover, they are knowledgeable of the importance to contribute to the welfare and prosperity of humanity.

The suffering of people anywhere is a problem to humanitarians everywhere. Physical distance is not a barrier to emotional discontent about man's inhumanity to man. Gender discrimination and disempowerment of women are no exception. These remain as scourges of women in the modern world. In order for us to improve women's lives and reduce children's suffering, morally weak men and unjust society must be prevailed upon to forswear the acid of sexist attitudes and patriarchal customs. Until then, women's fundamental rights and liberty will never be fully respected and equally guaranteed. It is axiomatic that human rights should be universally observed as the birthright of every human being.

Many men and societies have yet to act as befits the human dignity and democratic civilisation they proclaimed for themselves. It is only proper of civilised humans to establish relationships that are devoid of resentment, hostility, and dissension. As individuals, we must deal with each other on the basis of equality. It cannot be politic for civilised humans to hold a group of people inferior and the other superior on the basis of race or gender. Any gesture or conduct, writing or display, which incites violence or prejudicial action against humans can only be considered uncivilised. The same goes for anyone who carries out such amoralities.

There are those men of low morals who claim that women are inferior and less able than they are. About women there're no lack of bias and stereotype, no absence of ignorance and misconception. It is shocking that there are men who speak of women in the twenty-first century with discriminatory tones. Spurious beliefs that kept women socially and economically disadvantaged are all too pervasive. As a result, many human societies have proven to be an unsafe place for millions of women and girls to live, work, and play. Eliminating gender discrimination is the key to women's empowerment. In facing this challenge, feminists and womanitarians must strive, with combined strength, in the quest for gender equality. Male chauvinists can only be confounded by restoring to women their inherent dignity and inalienable rights. As for us, whose hopes for women are bright, we must dedicate ourselves for the realisation of a happier life for our sisters of the human family.

Chapter 1

Men's Traditional Sexist Views

F rom time immemorial, egotism, bigotry, intolerance, racism, and sexism have plagued human relations. These diseases reek of a society of favouritism, inequality, conflicts, hostilities, wars, and discriminatory practices . . . the amoral list goes on. Men's mal-ambitions for dominating others have incited them to do everything immoral towards this end. Egotistic men have always extended their efforts to become the masters of the fate of others. Self-proclaimed 'superiors' are notorious in sinking those who they considered as the least of humanity down to an inferior state of being in society. This practice has cast a dark shadow of amoral activities over the globe. Among these immoralities are disparagement and oppression.

Men are notorious egotists. To achieve their mal-desires, depraved men have committed many callous crimes, which have outraged the morally upright people of the world. Against women, alas, depraved men have heretofore and still are marginalising and mistreating them along the ideological lines of patriarchy, sexism, and male chauvinism. The basis of gender discrimination has been methodological in oppressing women. These untenable doctrines have hampered and weakened the usefulness and importance of women in society. Men who embrace those vice ideals have always had the attitude of contempt and disregard towards women.

1

Dictated to follow these sexist ideologies, morally weak men never cease to endeavour to detract women from their overall quality.

Sexist gestures and conducts are influential forces of evil practices in the world community. The spurious claims of women being less important and able than their male counterparts seem to occupy the thoughts of men everywhere. Even the major world religions have deprecated women to a certain extent. Gender discrimination and rights violations suffered by women and girls are not confined to any one age or nation. The vilification of women as inferior has been internalised by men of religion and cultural traditions throughout the ages the world over.

> Attitudes, beliefs and practices that serve to exclude women are often deeply entrenched, and in many instances closely associated with cultural, social and religious norms. Surveys, opinion polls and case studies provide a good indication of the prevalence of gender discrimination in many countries.
>
> A Gallup Poll conducted in five Latin American countries (Argentina, Brazil, Colombia, El Salvador and Mexico) found that half of the respondents believed society favours men over women. In Brazil, only 20 per cent of respondents, both men and women, believe that society treats both sexes equally, while more than half of respondents in that country, and in neighbouring Argentina, consider that women and men do not enjoy equal job opportunities.[1]

---

[1]   *The State of the World's Children*, 2007, 8

We must be mindful also that bias attitudes and spurious beliefs are not only shared by men, but by misguided women who have yet to understand their true potentials, qualities, and values.

> The survey revealed that women's views can also be equally discriminatory towards their own sex, if not quite as extreme. A surprisingly large number of women respondents from the survey agreed or strongly agreed with the statement that men make better political leaders than women—including over half of women respondents from Bangladesh, China, Islamic Republic of Iran and Uganda, over one third from Albania and Mexico, and one out of every five from the United States. This underlines the fact that discriminatory attitudes towards women and girls are not simply held by men, but also reflect norms and perceptions that may be shared by the entire society.[2]

If discriminatory practices are to become history, then gender myths and ignorance must first be eliminated. Education, understanding, goodwill, tolerance, and feminism are required to rid the world of sexist attitudes and customs. Being detrimental to women and girls, no religion or cultural tradition can rightfully justify inequality and disempowerment. Traditional stereotypes towards women have formed the basis of men's action across the globe. Women have and will always be oppressed by sexist traditions. Consequently, *they* have long existed under the most difficult and oppressive predicaments. This is due to men's historic traditional sexist views. But no morally civilised man will take pride in practicing violence or prejudicial actions against women. These acts of disregard have merely resulted in brutality, inhumanity, and viciousness against women. They deprive women of their inherent dignity, equity, freedom, and thus inalienable rights.

---

[2] *The State of the World's Children*, 2007, 8

Chapter 3

Women in the Modern World

Women's groups have launched some effective attacks on sexism and patriarchy. The achievements that have been made opposing violations and deprivations of women's rights are remarkable. As a result, the modern world offers great potential to assure women's rights and to improve their lot. Within the modern context of a just society, all humans are to be treated on a non-discriminatory basis regardless of race, ethnicity, religion, gender, or any other distinction. Women are today far better off than their predecessors in terms of access to health care, protection, education, and employment. But there yet remains far to go in ridding the world of the nefarious practices of discrimination. Patriarchal societies and sexist individuals, in their ignorance, continue to marginalise the rights and interests of millions of women. These oppressed women are confronted by daily challenges and violations of their human rights.

For millions of women and girls, unfortunately, the twenty-first-century experience is one of poverty, stereotypes, abuse, and exclusion. Human rights abuses are linked with so many girls not being protected and educated. In April of the 14th year of the twenty-first century, for instance, Boko Haram gunmen abducted approximately 300 female students from the Government Secondary School in the town of Chibok in Borno State, Nigeria. It is feared that many of the schoolgirls have been forced to convert to Islam and others sold into marriages and sexual slavery. However, this is not only about Nigeria; it is crucial to protect the rights of every girl everywhere. We should not wait for a similar abduction to take place before raising our collective voice for action to protect the safety and rights of girls. The failure to do so will merely link to further human rights abuses against adolescent girls.

The risk of such abuses will increase if greater value is not placed on the worth of women and girls as human beings. Fresh impetus should be given to the cause to take comprehensive measures to protect females from all forms of violence. Those who are poor are most likely to suffer discrimination. Social and traditional barriers still impede millions of females to enjoy their inherent right to non-discrimination. This should serve to remind us of the urgent imperative of our time to strive for the true implementation of the measures necessary to ensure sameness of opportunities and rights for all people. Eroding all forms of discrimination is requisite in the establishment of true equality among members of the human family.

Equality is vital today because of the immense moral progress that it will accelerate our modern world towards. Discriminatory practices are poisonous to the welfare, well-being, and prosperity of women. We should abhor every unprincipled act, which is an insult to the modernity of human civilisation. Scientific and technological advancement of highly urbanised and industrialised societies are not full evidence of being civilised. A hard line against inhumane, unethical, and unreasonable practices is indispensable to the moral and intellectual advancement of being civilised. However, let us not be bemused by legislated equality. Institutionalised partiality against women still goes on unchallenged. Therefore, more attempts must be made to be rid of such nefariousness wherever it is found and in whatever guise it is met. This will assure freedom and equality for the millions of women to whom it is still denied.

No one can morally deny that human rights abuses against women and girls have no place in a civilised world. Moreover, a world that fails to take a hard line against gender-based violence and discrimination is not fit for women and their children.

> A world fit for children is also a world fit for women. They are inseparable and indivisible—one cannot exist without the other. Lofty ambitions, good intentions and catchy slogans will not produce human progress. The road to sustainable development cannot be paved with half measures. Sound investments and a resolute commitment to justice, gender equality and children are required. If all citizens are allowed the opportunity to reach their potential, then nations will thrive. No argument against gender equality, whether based on traditions, customs or outright bigotry, can disprove the claim that women's rights are good for children and ultimately good for the world.[3]

Today, millions of women are affected by deeply entrenched gender-based prejudice and stereotypes. It is vital to tackle the root causes of human rights abuses against women and girls. More women need to gain power over their lives. Disempowered women tend to have fewer rights and fewer opportunities to reach their full potential. Domestic violence, discrimination, poverty, and inequalities are among the biggest barriers for women to overcome in order to secure their children's well-being. To do this, the masses of the world must align with womanitarianism.

---

[3]   *The State of the World's Children*, 2007, 15

Chapter 4

The Vile Doctrine: Male Chauvinism

M ale chauvinism actually perceives females as a biological defect. This false doctrine simply denigrates women in its mal-belief that they are inferior to men. Male chauvinists actually posit women to receive less than equal treatment or benefit to men. In contrary to this vile doctrine, the mere biological differences between men and women are their sex chromosomes (structure in living cells).

> The call for equal rights evolved into a quest for gender equality when a distinction was made between gender and sex. Sex is biological: Females have two X chromosomes and males have one X and one Y chromosome. Gender, on the other hand, is a social construct that describes what is feminine and what is masculine. Recognizing that gender roles are not inborn but rather learned, proponents of gender equality challenged the stereotypes and pervasive discrimination that kept women and girls socially and economically disadvantaged.[4]

---

[4]   *The State of the World's Children*, 2007, 1

But in spite of these challenges, women and girls are yet to be free from gender-based mistreatments. Male chauvinists simply lack regards for the fundamental human rights, the dignity, and the worth of women. All knowledgeable people know that gender is not a source of superiority or inferiority. It is truism that a male generally has a larger physique in comparison to the average woman. But it is equally true that women are not innately less important, intelligent, or able than men. Male chauvinism is the ringleader in the discrimination and disempowerment of women. It underlines the misogyny of hatred towards women. The respect which this vile doctrine lacks for human rights is the one that is essential in eliminating discriminations and empowering women and girls.

To denote fondness, love, or admiration for women, actually, does not merely mean promiscuousness. The philosophy of philogyny can also be articulate through feminism and womanitarianism. There is a long-standing need in the world for correcting those misconceptions which hinder women to attain similar prospect as men. Nothing less than full equality of all members of society is needed to assure a perfect utopia. Equality is indeed a good augury for tolerance, peace, and harmony among humans.

More people need to become sensible to the fact that denigration and disparagement only result in trials and vicissitudes in the life of humans. Only people of low morals embrace the vile isms that incite violence and prejudicial actions against others. Male chauvinism is a product of enmity and violence towards women. Sexism laid women as easy prey to be patronized and disparaged. Anti-feminism is a driving wedge in the disparities between women and men. Discrimination, in all its forms, is immoral. Humans are all interdependent and, therefore, are no less important to each other. Inequality is unacceptable in every context. Misogynists only hinder women and girls to be freed from human rights abuses.

Anti-feminism only pollutes the atmosphere of society with sexist stance. There is no safety for women and children in an atmosphere reeking with the vileness of male chauvinism and misogyny. Gender discrimination is very perilous to the prospects of women and children—especially girls. Favouritism towards boys is unsatisfactory for the prospect of girls.

> Gender discrimination is pervasive. While the degrees and forms of inequality may vary, women and girls are deprived of equal access to resources, opportunities and political power in every region of the world. The oppression of girls and women can include the preference for sons over daughters, limited personal and professional choices for girls and women, the denial of basic human rights and outright gender-based violence.
>
> Inequality is always tragic and sometimes fatal. Prenatal sex selection and infanticide, prevalent in parts of South and East Asia, show the low value placed on the lives of girls and women and have led to unbalanced populations where men outnumber women.
>
> Despite overall growth in educational enrolment, more than 115 million children of primary school age do not receive an elementary education. With few exceptions, girls are more likely than boys to be missing from classrooms across the developing world. Girls who do enrol in school often drop out when they reach puberty for many reasons—the demands of household responsibilities, a lack of school sanitation, a paucity of female role models, child marriage or sexual harassment and violence, among others.[5]

---

[5]   *The State of the World's Children*, 2007, 6–7

Chapter 6

Women's Betterment

At this moment in time, we must give due regard to problems affecting womankind. Everyone should, by now, be concerned about the major challenges confronting women throughout the world. We must seize the initiatives to work for the preservation of the integrity of femininity and the better treatment of women. Only those who lack forethought have and will fail to take a stand to ensure that the fundamental human rights of women are safeguarded and guaranteed.

In most societies, women are the cornerstone that keeps the family structure together. Women generally play the most pivotal role in children upbringing. As with most of us, my mother, Doreen McKenzie (née Edgehill), played the most significant role in my upbringing. Furthermore, my maternal grandmother, Winnifred Edgehill (née Williams) (1932–1998), was the one who taught me to read at age 12 in the summer of 1996, teaching me to spell and pronounce labels on food items in her small grocery shop. Of this I am certain: women generally taught their young ones the basic skills of survival such as cooking, ironing, washing, and cleanliness. In all probability, you can relate to this reality. It is fitting for all women to be protected against the age-old problems, which blight their prospects of a happy life.

Although women are our life carriers and thus mothers of human posterity, it is amoral of those who endeavour to consign them to a life of motherhood and domesticity. Like men, women have ambitions and potentials to be whatever they desire. But historically, the individual views and opinions of men about women are often too shallow. As a result, each passing generation of men, ignobly, failed to give thoughtful consideration for women's well-being and prosperity. Men must open their eyes and broaden their views regarding the welfare of women. And to do this, they must be prevailed upon to understand that besides their own inherent rights and interests, there are those of women that should be respected.

It is in this realisation that both genders can coexist harmoniously with each other. For a relationship without the virtues of tolerance, understanding, goodwill, and respect is like a house that is built on sand—it will inevitably be destroyed. It is axiomatic that everyone would benefit from a better social and interpersonal relationship. The advanced progress of a just society must be made in the development of respect for the opposite genders. Any attempt to fully respect the human rights of only one gender will, inevitably, belittle those of the other. This only creates gender-based partialities and disparities in the overall structure of the society. This is an undeniable reality. If moral faculty in men cannot be awakened and focused on the problems which befall women each day, mankind will bequeath to their daughter and their daughter's daughter a lifetime of subordination and indignant unhappiness. Like men, thankfully, there are women who will die in defence of their human rights.

All of us need to become dedicated to the betterment of the conditions of women's living standard. We all know the wretchedness and subordination of those women who are denied of their inherent dignity, equality, and their inalienable rights. Improvement of their living standards and the advancement of women's rights must be achieved. For a woman that is denigrated, insecure, and unhappy will take no pride in her existence as a

> These words link equality to human development, recognizing that both women and men are essential for the social and economic progress of nations. More than 60 years ago, global leaders envisioned a world where all people shared equally in rights, resources and opportunities, where abundance ruled and every man, woman and child was free from despair and inequity.[7]

The theoretical standards for human rights have also been raised by the International Covenant on Civil and Political Rights 1966 and the International Covenant on Economic, Social and Cultural Rights 1966. Based on the ideas that relate to the inalienable fundamental rights to which every human being is inherently entitled to, several regional treaties have been conceived. These include the European Convention on Human Rights (ECHR) 1950; the American Convention on Human Rights 1969; African Charter on Human and Peoples' Rights (also known as the Banjul Charter) 1981; and the Arab Charter on Human Rights 2004. Regional human rights regimes affirm the principles enshrined in the UN's Universal Declaration of Human Rights and the international covenants on human rights.

The human rights instruments of the United Nations Charter contained the essential principles for the preservation of world peace, improvement of the education level of the world, ameliorate world poverty, and eliminate global violations of human rights. However, decades have elapsed since the United Nations General Assembly adopted UDHR in 1948. Although member states have pledged themselves to achieve, in cooperation with the United Nations, the promotion of the Charter, universal equality is still absent among humans. The pervasiveness of gender discrimination that women face throughout their lives is a testament to the fact.

---

[7]   *The State of the World's Children*, 2012, 1

The fundamental rights and status enjoyed by many women today, actually, was not achieved overnight. In retrospect, it took decades before UDHR extended its emphasis on the human rights of women and children. The United Nations' heed to the calls for a proclamation relating to women's rights was not answered until 1974. This came twenty-eight years after the UN Commission on the Status of Women (CSW), which was established in 1946 to monitor the situation of women worldwide and promote women's rights in all societies. During its first session in 1947, the commission declared as one of its guiding principles

> to raise the status of women, irrespective of nationality, race, language or religion, to equality with men in all fields of human enterprise, and to eliminate all discrimination against women in the provisions of statutory law, in legal maxims or rules, or in interpretation of customary law.

The work of CSW has resulted in a number of important declarations and conventions that protect and promote the human rights of women. Owing to CSW, the UN General Assembly adopted the Convention on the Elimination of All Forms of Discrimination against Women (CEDAW) in 1979, which entered into force on 3 September 1981. The Convention on the Rights of the Child (CRC), which focuses on the inalienable rights of children, was adopted in 1989 and took effect on 2 September 1990.

The inalienable fundamental rights of women are vital to the satisfactory state of children being healthy and happy.

> Since the status of women and the well-being of children are deeply intertwined, advocates for children would be remiss if they failed to champion the cause of gender equality. The Convention on the Elimination of all Forms

of Discrimination against Women . . . and the Convention on the Rights of the Child . . . are sister treaties—inexorably linked in moving communities towards full human rights. Each delineates specific entitlements that cannot be abrogated due to age, gender, economic class or nationality. The two treaties are complementary, overlapping in their call for precise rights and responsibilities and filling in crucial gaps that may exist when either stands alone.

Several articles of CEDAW address rights pertinent to children, including equality (articles 2 and 15), protecting maternity (article 4), adequate health care (article 12) and shared parental responsibility (article 16). The CRC calls for equal access for girls and boys to education and health care. Both conventions demand freedom from violence and abuse and are based on principles of non-discrimination, participation and accountability.

The treaties are not perfectly harmonious: There are areas of tension. For instance, some supporters of gender equality believe that the CRC stereotypes women as mothers, limiting their life options. Some child rights advocates think that CEDAW focuses too much on a woman's right to self-actualization and may unintentionally subvert the importance of motherhood. Despite these differences, the two conventions hold more in common than in opposition—they set the standards for an equitable world in which the rights of every human being—female and male, old and young—are respected.[8]

---

[8] *The State of the World's Children*, 2012, 2–3

Despite the womanitarian and egalitarian sentiments of those conventions for women and children, all nations have yet to fully accept and ratify them. In fact, CEDAW has received 187 ratifications, accessions, and successions by states parties. The United States of America, Sudan, Somalia, and Iran has all failed to do so. CRC has received 193. Yet again, the United States of America, Somalia, and South Sudan have all failed to sign this convention.

Because of disregard and contempt for those treaties, millions of women and girls throughout the world remain powerless, voiceless, and without rights. It is clear that the United Nations General Assembly have adopted numerous international covenants to promote political, economic, civil, social, and educational rights of women and children. It is also obvious that much more still needs to be done to change the attitude of the world towards equality. It does help when so many member states fail to keep the basic principles of the UN Declaration of Human Rights constantly in mind—to strive to promote respect for the rights and freedom of women and children.

Brazil, China, Canada, Egypt, France, Germany, India, Italy, Malaysia, New Zealand, the Netherlands, South Korea, Singapore, Spain, the United Kingdom, Venezuela . . . the list goes on.

Can you imagine! So many modern states have strongly objected to measures to ensure women's civil, political, economic, and cultural rights and their legal equality. It is axiomatic that patriarchal world leaders detest the principles of equality and non-discrimination that has been embodied in the UN's democratic conventions. Because of those states' refusal to accept completely the UN provisions to eliminate gender discrimination, various issues concerning women's rights still exist in all areas of life. These reservations merely weaken the UN institution and procedures which serve as the Universal Declaration of Human Rights and blunt its international instruments of the Convention on the Elimination of All Forms of Discrimination against Women.

It is a moral crime on the part of those nations that are now locked in a stalemate with the UN to accept completely the ideals enshrined in the Charter to ensure the full and equal enjoyment by women of all human rights and fundamental freedoms and to take effective action to prevent violations of these rights. Nations disregard for CEDAW and CRC have left millions of women and girls with no other choice than to cope with the paucity of equal rights to men and boys.

It has been over thirty years since CEDAW was adopted by the United Nations.

One can only imagine what the lives of girls born in 1979 would have been like had the convention been fully supported and implemented. A generation of empowered women would have made a world of difference. As a Chinese adage says, 'Women hold up half the sky.' The next generation cannot wait another three decades for its rights. Women and girls must have the means and support to fulfil their potential and fully enjoy their rights.[9]

---

[9]   *The State of the World's Children*, 2007, 15

Chapter 10

Stop Devaluing Women in Society

There are many towers of misanthropic ideas that have been erected in human societies against women. These towers of hatred and ignorance are in dire need to be demolished. Unprincipled ideologies that do not consider women important as men, in all moral sense, have no place in civilised societies. But misogynists in their unremitting sexist attitude have ensured the futility of the ideals of feminism. Owing to the ignoble attitude of men, the basket of women in society is overflowing with nothing but issues just waiting to be resolved.

It is quite unfortunate that women are still at a disadvantage throughout the world. It is shocking, to say the least, that even in the twenty-first century men still fail to realise the fact that members of both genders are important to the viable functioning of society. The rights and interests of all members of the human race should be valued equally. But male chauvinists are notorious in neglecting that fact to undermine the importance and value of women in society, denying them their human liberty. This leaves hundreds of millions of women dependent on their husband/boyfriend or welfare benefit. And for those women who desire to fend for themselves with the aim of being independent, the constraint on their opportunity leaves them no other choice but to adapt to subservient roles in society. Unfortunately, this world does not hold in high esteem women in subservient positions and those that are dependent. Society tends to look down on dependent women, even those on welfare benefits.

In view of facts, one can say that it doesn't seem to be sheer coincidence why the rank, dignity, and significance of women are predominantly degraded. I believe that this has been done deliberately to justify the inferior theory of women. There seems to be a rooted gynophobia of empowered women in human societies. In consequence of such abnormal fear of women, the limitation and denial of women's rights and prospects are deeply entrenched in human societies throughout the world. As a direct result, the abasement of women is the inevitable outcome. Pervasive anti-feminist societies provide tangible evidence to substantiate my claim of the gynophobia of empowered women. That is preposterous! If there is anyone we should be afraid of, it should be men, who for centuries have and continue to play havoc with humanity. For example, depraved men are infamous for committing the licentious crimes of rape/sexual assault, physical and verbal abuse against women and girls. This is exactly why so many women have understandably developed androphobia and misandry.

Women do feel the full brunt of man's inhumanity to them. It is the norm for some cultures to consider the act of making the importance or status of women secondary to men. Can you imagine that the refusal to allow women to be truly valued has been considered appropriate? All acts of devaluing of women must undergo considerable changes in every modern society. Until this is fully realised, men will continue treating women as the dregs of society/humanity. As long as the morally inappropriate gestures and conducts that are aimed in the direction of women continue to be ignored and approved of by society, the poor quality of women's will forever be adulterated with injustice and oppression.

It is true that every society has its own mores and culture. It is also true that there are understandable differences in gender roles, dress codes, and behaviour in almost every human society. It is also common of every society to teach girls and boys the traditional customs and ways of behaving that are typical of each gender. So from an early age, children learn to accustom themselves to the overall culture and what is expected of them by society. However, it is normal of most cultures to posit that men should play a dominant role in society. But traditionally, women have been demeaned and badly scourged by the dominance of men. There are many evidences of this even in the modern world. Take the workforce for example; it has been continuously dominated by men. Owing to traditional stereotypes against women, there are strictures on women's choice of career. This only blunts the employment prospects of millions of women. But upon moral grounds, there is nothing, and I mean nothing, that can justify the age-old 'it's a man's job' or 'it's a woman's job' theories. It can only be justified morally for an individual, without regards to his or her gender, to be employed because of career choices and not according to society's stereotypes. Therefore, if a woman desires to work in the construction industry and if a man desires to work as a nurse, so be it.

Women who do traditional so-called male jobs are not something of a rarity though. This is because of the great awakening of many societies by the cardinal fact that women are not inherently handicap in doing the same job as men. In fact, women have proved to be just as effective as men in the workforce. This reaffirms my belief in the need for human societies to stop imposing certain gender roles in the workforce particularly. This is bad for the society and the economy with an end result of low employment rate of women. It is precisely unjust and a stupid mistake of any society to limit or barricade a particular group of people from entering the workforce to labour for their honest bread.

The importance and value of women should be taken very seriously. Furthermore, I think that women are more compassionate than men, and thereby, they should play a more dominant role in the heart of our societies. For a long time, the dominance of men was thought to be the best thing for society. But we now have proof to the contrary. The ascendency of men has prevailed as the scourge of the world. Simply, the uncompassionate and merciless global governance of men has led to enslavement, wars, environmental degradation, impoverishment, and exploitation. History has produced evidence in substantiation of the fact that men have fought many battles and even went to the ends of the earth to annex land and pillage the natural resources of indigenous people around the globe. It is a historic tendency of men who acquire high status to abuse their authority to dominate every aspect of society and the world at large. As a result of this, humanity has experienced many grim days.

Regardless of where they live, the value of women in this world is often demeaned by sexist norms. Obviously, the debasement of women is one of the major problems which ignite the fire of burden into the lives of millions. In spite of the difference of race and creed between women in this world, they all love to be valued and respected. The unprincipled ideals which debase the value of women must be rid of from human societies. It's a disgrace that the worth of women is all too often defiled by society's ignoble customs. It is, therefore, noble of those who voice their opinions and express solidarity against the devaluing of women in society.

Furthermore, children's rights are more likely
to be realised when women fully enjoy their
social and economic rights. Policymakers are
becoming attuned to the reality that women have
an important economic role in addressing the
poverty experienced by children; an increasing
number of countries are channelling provisions
to fulfil children's rights—such as cash transfers
contingent on sending children to school—directly
to mothers. Across the world, the livelihoods of
households are already often sustained and
enhanced by women who work outside the
home—from those who cultivate subsistence
crops or work on large farms where they oversee
the output and marketing of produce, to those
labouring in factories and offices. In both the
Caribbean and sub-Saharan Africa, for example,
women produce about 80 per cent of household
food consumed.[10]

---

[10]   *The State of the World's Children*, 2007, 37

Chapter 12

Equality Protects Women in the Workplace

I t is quite tangible that low earnings only leads to women owning fewer assets than men. Gender biases expose women to risk of violence, abuse, and poverty.

At work, women are often victimized by discrimination. They may be excluded from more highly remunerated occupations and are frequently paid less than men for the same work. Women and girls are often recruited into domestic work outside their own homes and may be forced to live away from their families, at times in oppressive, dangerous conditions. Destitute women and girls may find the sex trade their only option for employment when all other economic doors have been shut.

Ending the wage gap, opening higher-paying fields to women and allowing female workers more decision-making power will greatly benefit children. As women become economically productive, their spheres of influence increase.

They become able to make choices not only for themselves, but also for their children.

When a woman brings income or assets into the household, she is more likely to be included in decisions on how the resources will be distributed. Historically, when women hold decision-making power, they see to it that their children eat well, receive adequate medical care, finish school and have time for recreation and play. Women who have access to meaningful, income-producing work are more likely to increase their families' standards of living, leading children out of poverty.[11]

If we are honest to our forethought for a perfect utopia, then we will give effective attention to measures necessary to bring to fruition the total liberty and equality of women to men. It is insignificant to speculate about the problems of women. For there is one truth—that women confront daily challenges and violations of their human rights. Equality is essential in protecting women against the indignities and injustices they face in the workplace. Equality in the workplace is necessary to assess women's progress. But in order to promote gender equality, poverty reduction, and sustainable development of the lot of women, undoubtedly, the deeply ingrained bias attitudes and cultural beliefs must be rid from society.

---

[11]   *The State of the World's Children*, 2007, 13

Chapter 13

The Double Burden

Throughout history, the desire to dominate, so connected with men, has been a catalyst for hostilities and inequalities among humans. Today, as in the past, men are widely regarded as the most fitting breadwinners of their families. Yet there are millions of women shouldering the bulk of the responsibilities to provide the basic necessities for their families. In fact, hundreds of millions of women today, as in the past, are entrusted with most of the day-to-day responsibilities in the raising of children. Women are the most typical primary caregivers in both nuclear and single-parent families.

Traditional gender ideologies have posited women as caregivers and men as breadwinners. But men commonly fail to be the providers for their families, while women are least likely to abdicate their responsibilities of caring for their young ones. As an example, there are more single mothers than fathers struggling with the heavy workloads of the double burden—working to earn money but also have responsibility for unpaid domestic labour. People do not need any statistics but simply look about their vicinity where they may find a few, if any, single fathers in this situation. When parents are separated or divorced, children have been less likely to live with their fathers. Some women are single mothers by choice, while others are not. In the case of parental separation, although the

41

law generally favours women the child's custody, very few men have and will voluntarily accept the responsibility of being a single father. In addition, some men are renowned to discontinue playing their fatherly roles in the upbringing of their child/children as soon as they're no longer in an intimate relationship with the mothers.

Even in nuclear family structures, nonetheless, when both parents are in full-time employment, mothers generally do more of the domestic workload than fathers. There is evidence to substantiate that women are working more but earning less than men.

> Whether they live in industrialized or developing countries, in rural or urban settings, in general, women work longer hours than men. While data on the way men and women use their time are sparse, surveys conducted in recent years confirm the validity of this assertion across developing countries. Oxfam estimates that women work around 60 to 90 hours per week, and time-use surveys reveal that across a selection of developing countries in Asia, Latin America and sub-Saharan Africa, women's working hours exceed those of men, often by a wide margin.

> For many women, unpaid chores in and for the household take up the majority of their working hours, with much less time spent in remunerative employment. Data from urban areas in 15 Latin American countries reveal that unpaid household work is the principal activity for 1 in every 4 women; the corresponding ratio for men is 1 in every 200. Even when they participate in the labour market for paid employment, women still undertake the majority of work in the home. Here again, this finding is substantiated by research in countries across developing regions. In Mexico, for example, women in paid employment also perform

household tasks that absorb 33 hours of their time each week; in contrast, men's contribution to domestic chores amounts to just 6 hours per week.

Time-use surveys in six states in India reveal that women typically spend 35 hours per week on household tasks and caring for children, the sick and elderly, against 4 hours per week for men. The division of household labour is not dissimilar in industrialized countries. Although gender disparities in the overall work burden are less marked than in developing countries, women in the more affluent nations still spend a far greater proportion of working hours than men in unpaid work. Despite the limited time that many women spend in paid employment and their pivotal contribution to the functioning of the household, there is a widespread view that women as well as men should contribute to household income. Findings from the World Values Survey reveal that when asked whether husbands and wives should both contribute to household income, a clear majority of respondents agreed—around 90 per cent on average in countries surveyed in East Asia and Pacific, Latin America, sub-Saharan Africa and transition economies, and more than two thirds in the Middle East and South Asia.[12]

The ideologies of traditional gender roles play a pivotal part in this worldwide injustice. Some men rather add to the stress of the workload around the house for the women than help. As a simple example, there are those men who will not even wash-up the dishes much less clean the house. To them, assumingly, household cleanliness is a 'woman's job'. But only minds that are morally dirty are misled down that path.

---

[12]   *The State of the World's Children*, 2007, 37–38

Consequently, those misguided men leave the average woman in the household spending more time than man dealing with childcare and housework. Women are more likely to carry out, without choice, the domestic side of the burdens. But it is only morally proper for couples to shoulder the double burden fair and square—especially if both partners are in paid jobs. It is only when men are guided by upright morality they can acquire the necessary knowledge to understand the importance of being fair to women and vice versa.

It is important that humans live a balanced life that is so necessary to our well-being. It is only when an individual maintains a work–life balance that he or she can have enough time for work and enough to have a life. Similarly, people must maintain a work–family balance to strike an even balance between their occupational lives with their family lives. Gender equality furthers the balance and increase child survival and proper development. Empowered and happy women are more likely to produce healthy babies. As women are the primary caregivers for children, the well-being of their offspring are often determined by that of the mothers. The primary caregivers, women, must gain the full autonomy to control their own lives and to participate in making decisions that affect them and their families. By implementing the bill of women's rights, societies would definitely redress the balance between man and woman.

Traditional sexist ideologies have rendered women defenceless to dangers ranging from violence, exploitation to oppression, discrimination, and disempowerment. This is attributed to the scarcity of equal work for both parents in raising children. Sexist ideologies only marginalized women in society. Women are vulnerable to the misconceptions of gender roles. Every disadvantaged woman is a victim of sexism. And every oppressed and disempowered woman is a victim of male chauvinism. More needs to be done to secure the rights and liberties of all women, wherever they live, wherever they are subordinated and taken for granted. We womanitarians can, and must, thrive to overcome the barriers that have kept women from living a more productive and happier life.

Chapter 14

Religious Subordination of Women

No one can deny that the greatest ethical rules and regulations created by humans to make society obedient to godliness and to avoid evil are those associated with religion. It is correct to say, therefore, that one of the essences of religion dictates good influences. In time of toil and hardship, it has brought comfort and ease to the most faithful in their trials and tribulations. Religion has brought great spiritual and moral dividends to society and those who use it for good purposes. But it has always brought harm to humanity by those who use it for the evil purpose of damnation.

From the most primitive times to modern civilisation, religion has served *humans for both good and evil purposes*. Religious bigotry has been a notorious obstacle in the coming together of people of all diverse faith. Religious teachings not only inspire reverence for God and fellowship of believers but also incite passion—causing self-righteousness, bigotry, and dogmatism. These acts are carried out by religious bigots who do not know the true values of righteousness, which is godliness—opposing unrighteousness and immoralities. History teaches that wherever there are religious mal-perceptions, there is always disharmony, conflict, hostility, and social injustice.

In order to follow righteousness, however, human civilization grew around religion. But to make women obedient to patriarchal traditions and sexist customs, male chauvinists have incorporated their ungodly ideologies in their religious beliefs. As a result, religion can be a heavenly sanctuary and hellish experience for women. Most, if not all, religions practise gender inequality at many levels such as worship, governance, and education. In some religions, for instance, women are not allowed to become spiritual leaders or to pray alongside men. Because of gender bias in religion, *men* have always played the most important part in leading worship, while women have been confined to more passive roles. It is only when human practices are guided by sexism women are made dependent, secondary, and subservient to men. Only those religious teachings which promote moral decency, peace, equality, chivalry, and tolerance can be considered *good influences*. But gender subordination is an ungodly influence with the end result being the debasement of women's dignity and fundamental worth.

Men are infamous to proclaim their evil purposes to dominate as 'God's will'. Their subordination of women is no exception. Credulous people cherish many falsehoods and misconceptions about God. Many of these lies and *con-cepts* were actually written by ancient scribes. The wise will accept the fact that no wholly good god will approve of injustices and cruelty. A perfect god will forbid discrimination and favouritism towards any gender. But reality shows that the godly claims in many religions are often highly controversial. In the doctrine of creationism, for example, the creation of women was actually a secondary thought of God.

According to biblical creationists, for instance, 'he' apparently created every living creature before creating the woman, Eve, from 'a single rib' of Adam, the man. This is clearly exemplified in Genesis 2. On the contrary, in Genesis 1:26–27, the scribe actually claimed that God said, 'Let us make mankind in our own image, in our likeness; so that they may have dominion over the fish of the sea, and over the fowls of the air, and over the cattle, and over all the earth, and over every creeping thing that creeps upon the earth. So God created mankind in his own image; male and female he created them.'

This merely contradicts the later clams in Genesis 2. Clearly, according to these biblical passages of Genesis 1, mankind is used in a gender-neutral aspect. Secondly, mankind (woman and man) was created in the image of God. Therefore, such god must be androgynous and thus having both male and female features. Or the speaking deity was addressing a multiracial (as humans are) group of god and goddess. He must've been communicating with at least one other person to have instructed 'let *us* make mankind in *our* own image, in *our* likeness . . .' Thirdly, however, man and woman were created at the same time, with equal domination over the earth and all living things that dwell therein. This is also clearly exemplified in Genesis 1:28–31, where God gave them his blessing to 'be fruitful and multiply and fill the earth'.

Besides the creation story, there is another controversial and contradicting passage regarding women in Genesis 3. To be precise, this is the biblical account of how sin came in this world. To add insult to injury, the woman, Eve, is blamed for this. In short, ironically a 'talking snake' allegedly persuaded Eve to pick and eat fruits from God's forbidden fruit tree in the centre of the Garden of Eden. She also gave Adam the forbidden fruits to eat. And in his displeasure of this, God put some terrible curses not only on Eve but also on her offspring as well. Apparently, the pains of childbirth and the dominion of men over women is allegedly a part of God's curse on Eve. Anyone who believes this would believe anything.

It is fair to say that there have been and still remain men who act as if God did not create them. But instead, it is rather them who had created God in their own image and likeness and bestowed upon themselves dominion over those who they consider the least.

Anyway, I personally denounce both the stories of creationism and evolution theories. I have said this in the conviction that no one, no matter how educated or how persuasive his or her narrative or argument, can tell, without controversy, how the world began and how all living things first came to inhabit it. It is evident that every doctrine that tries to decode the beginning not only contradicts each other but also themselves. Owing to the lack of eyewitness accounts, no doubt, the mystery of the beginning is insoluble.

The historic subordination of women in religions, moreover, articulates how women were viewed in ancient times. Religious mistreatment of women provides an account to the chauvinistic opinions of ancient scribes. Although the traditional ideologies of each religion vary in the restriction of women, the fundamental factors of equality needs to be awakened in each. Religious believers must come to the cardinal realisation that both men and women are equally capable to carry out certain tasks. Religion, as proclaimed to be 'a symbol of peace and godliness', should only guide and inspire humans to adhere to good morality and to live in love and unity with each other—without any regards whatsoever.

The teachings of any wholly good god are based upon peace, harmony, and equality. These must be the abiding grace of God. In Christianity for example, this cardinal fact is evident for all to read in 2 Corinthians 3:17, 'Where the Spirit of the Lord is, there is liberty.' Then God must be absent from every Christian state that practises the nefariousness of inequalities and oppression. To invoke the spirit of God, the wholly good one, all the world's major religions should contemplate struggling for equality, human rights, and world peace. *Righteousness*, so closely tied to religion, is not a meaningless word that is devoid of moral significance. It is a great philosophy that is devoid of compromise for unrighteousness and ungodliness. It is a philosophy that demands self-respect and, at the same time, equal respect for the legitimate beliefs and human dignity of others. Where the true principles of righteousness are not lacking, the equality of genders is assured at all levels.

These are the days when men of religion must come to the realisation that they must endeavour to uplift not only their spiritual and physical standard alone but those of others. There is nothing more rightful of godly people than to bring prosperity, equality, justice, happiness, peace, and well-being to those to whom it is denied. Of this, any wholly perfect and good god will approve.

Chapter 15

Household Inequality

We all know that the word *male* does not mean gender dominance. But the world is filled with male chauvinists who wish to rule and dominate women on the basis of gender. Through traditional stereotypes, society generally favours men over women as the head of the structure of the family. This social status is historically powered by income and assets. As a result, women are denied access to income-earning opportunities and ownership and management of assets. Empowered by patriarchal tyranny, men often have the strongest say in decision-making in the household. This only leaves women unequal and voiceless in their homes.

Household inequalities are influenced not only by income and assets but by age as well.

> The distribution of household bargaining power is also influenced by a woman's age at marriage and the age difference between a woman and her husband. Evidence from around the world shows that . . . when the age gap between spouses is most extreme, the burden of domestic work and childcare severely constrains the life choices available to married girls and child mothers. This,

in turn, affects the power that women have over household decisions.[13]

The unscrupulous factors that determine which family member will have the superior status in the household will never characterise the attitude of an individual who holds, in the highest esteem, the true ideals of equality. Regardless of who is older, who is the main breadwinner, or who is most educated, household decision-making cannot be rightly dominated by only one adult. Everyone should have an equal say. Because men have traditionally condemned this principle, women have and continue to be denied the rights to participate in major household decisions. To this extent, women are denied not only the rights to make major household purchases and daily household spending but also denied the rights in regard to their own health care and their visits with family or relatives outside of the household as well.

Anti-feminists seem to gain great satisfactions from the unhappy spectacle of women's disempowerment. Only a depraved man will be proud to espouse the ignoble restrictions of women. Men have, as a matter of following traditional mal-beliefs and not of moral principles, failed to realise that children are equally affected by problems that befall women. If the foes of gender parity redirect the staunch support which they have unfailingly given to the cause of the subjugation of women, they would grapple with the facts of how much they neglect the well-being of their children. No man today, no matter how persuasive his arguments, can morally justify the conducts that threaten the well-being and prosperity of women and children.

> The consequences of women's exclusion from household decisions can be as dire for children as they are for women themselves. In families in which women are key decision-makers, the

---

[13]   *The State of the World's Children*, 2007, 22

proportion of resources devoted to children
is far greater than in those in which women
have a less decisive role. This is because women
generally place a higher premium than men on
welfare-related goals and are more likely to use
their influence and the resources they control to
promote the needs of children in particular and
of the family in general. Case studies conducted
in the developing world indicate that women who
have greater influence in household decisions can
significantly improve their children's nutritional
status. Educating women also results in multiple
benefits for children, improving their survival
rates, nutritional status and school attendance.[14]

Unfortunately, in support of the age-old ignorance, the masses
of the world are so hesitant to condemn violations of women
fundamental rights. I am aware that like in the distant past, men
still oppress women to acquire the position of ascendancy in the
household. But I am also aware of the fact that the denials of those
birthrights of human freedom will never occur in the household of
a true man who adheres, strictly, to rightness. He will merely follow
the dictates of morally acceptable ideals which has a beneficent
effect on the welfare and well-being of his partner and their child/
children. True men are those who raise the standards of their
morale and that of their partners. They treat women with the same
principles by which they are willing to accept. Those upright men
will strive to make themselves happy, whilst at the same time, try to
make their partners happy as well.

The woman chosen, the house selected, the requirements imposed
for a happy home cannot be a hard line for the woman alone.
Equality and mutual respect are essential requirements to reach the
moral standard of a happy home for all. Love forms the basis of a

---

[14] *The State of the World's Children*, 2007, 23–24

good relationship, but respect, tolerance, and goodwill are vital to peaceful coexistence. Men who do not understand the importance of equality will find it difficult to see women as their equals. Gender inequality is an act of great malevolence. It is a long-standing obstacle to the happiness and empowerment of women in the household and society on a whole.

Chapter 16

Domestic Slavery

While we are sad at the oppression brought against women, there are men in their sexist ways who continue to impose the immorality of domestic bondage upon them. The state of being bound to the control of men is the abhorrent practices of which hundreds of millions of women have had to bear from ever since the days of yore. Women, who are not assertive or too weak to protect themselves, are all too often submissive to male chauvinists. So as long as women are restrained by their partners, they will always be consigned to a life of involuntary servitude within the household. When a woman finds herself in this unsatisfactory position, she has neither liberty of action nor freedom of will. She's, therefore, shackled and controlled by the will of her partner.

In the confines of the homes of many traditional nuclear families, millions of women have had to endure grave subjection. Those unfortunate women live an existence that is no less than being chattels or, in other words, slaves to their partners (masters). Oppression of women is amplified by a long history of male chauvinism and sexism. These have had a wretched impact on the lives of countless women. Without their conscious wishes, millions of women perform domesticated slavery across the globe. Having been oppressed for so long, unfortunately, many women have become inured to the subservient position in the household. These women are those who believe that they must be submissive to their husband/boyfriend.

Today, only a few ambitious women will settle happily into the servitude of domesticity. This brand of domestic slavery has been in practice for a very long time now. All forms of enslavement of women must be abolished. For as long as a woman is dedicated to combine work and family, her partner should not try to put her under any compulsion to do otherwise. The man should also accept his fair share of the responsibilities to help balance the parental and household duties. Furthermore, it is an act of a good parent, mother or father, to not allow work or any other duty schedules to leave him or her with very little time for parenting. Good partners encourage each other to chase their dreams. So instead of being a domestic slave master to his partner, a good man will rather give morale-boosting support to his partner to fulfil her ambitions.

There are those men who perform courtship display, ostensibly for a wife or girlfriend, but in actual fact to find a female chattel. There is evidence in many nuclear families where the so-called traditional breadwinners, as they're likely to be called, consigned their partners to a life of servitude and domesticity. This brand of domestic slavery is a violation of the human rights and dignity of women. As womanitarians, we must voice our opinions against these atrocious treatments in order to abolish domestic slavery, granting women true freedom.

All in all, to promote the unity and solidarity of our relationship, we must strive towards the mutuality of love, respect, and equality. People must complement each other to form good and lasting relationships. Therefore, we should never try to weaken the prospects of our partner. We must commit ourselves to the assurance of the eradication of every form of oppression and inequality from our relationships. We must ensure that our woman enjoys the great ideal of feminism in her home. In so doing, no doubt, we will raise the standards of equality and invoke the spirits of philogyny and philandry in our relationships. These principles are awesome prerequisites to a peaceably good relationship and a truly happy home.

A house will never be a home for a woman that is unhappy and live in constant fear of her life and well-being, therein. A woman will only be at home in a house where she is happy and confident that her partner will neither abuse her sexually, emotionally, physically, or verbally. Sexism has brought untold sorrow to womankind. Equal rights between men and women are vital to the establishment and maintenance of justice among the household. Respect for human welfare serves as the medium to ensure that a man and a woman live together in peace as true lovers. Men and women must live in unity and harmony.

Equality of men and women must be assured in the household. This will promote common interests for the good of the family. Every possibility must be explored to nurture the good and happy flowers of our relationship to blossom and bloom beautifully. Knowledgeable people know the viability of the household are not wholly in their hands. The stability of any nuclear family demands the united efforts of both mother and father. It is merely required of both parents to observe their obligations to the welfare of their children, their home, and to each other. Whenever the rights and interests of women are not assiduously observed as those of men, the prospect of a happy home becomes unattainable.

For far too long now, women's position in the household has been subservient to that of the average man. Whatever is considered chores in the home should no longer be a woman's job but a man's job as well. Because of sexist stereotypes, predominantly, women often find themselves in abusive or oppressive relationships. Acting as abolitionists, we must endeavour to stop the acts of domestic slavery. Efforts must also be extended to abolish that this brand of slavery in the home of the financial elite. It has been established that millions of women are pried away from their poor families to work as housekeepers in other countries for peanuts. To add insult to injury, their rich or wealthy employers often treat them very badly. It has been established that these slave masters (bosses) often keep these women at their beck and call—to do everything for them, no matter when or what they're asked to do. This only destroys the family structure and social aspect of women's life.

Domestic servitude is quite malevolent. Equality must be established in the household. Equal power must be vested in women and men.

> Women's access to power at the household level has the most direct impact on families and children. Here is where decisions are made about the allocation of resources for food, health care, schooling and other family necessities. When women are locked out of decisions regarding household income and other resources, they and their children are more likely to receive less food, and to be denied essential health services and education. Household chores, such as fetching water, gathering firewood or caring for the young or infirm, are delegated to mothers and daughters, which keeps them out of the paid labour force or school. When women share equally in household decisions, they tend to provide more adequately and fairly for their children.[15]

---

[15] *The State of the World's Children*, 2007, 12–13

Chapter 17

Evil Aggression: Domestic Violence

Although proclaimed highly moral and intellectually advanced, the entire human race is yet to forbid the immoralities which mar our societies today. Throughout the world, the principles of peace and harmony are constantly violated in human relations. People in their mindless endeavours arise many problems among each other. These issues are in dire need of solutions. Among these and still long outstanding is the millions of disadvantaged women. Time and again, it has been clearly demonstrated that the daily experience of millions of women is one of exclusion, abuse, and violence.

Mindlessness of domestic violence against women is today playing havoc in the lives of millions. This is an area in which the waves of feminist movements have thus far been unable to invoke its moral spirit to take effective actions. Domestic violence poses the gravest threat to women worldwide. Many societies have implemented measures to lessen the threat of amoralities against women. But violent males only fail to follow such ethical standards. It is a sad commentary on the millions of women that fall victim to the evil aggression of domestic violence. Domestic male aggressors are very harmful to the well-being of women and their children.

Heterosexual relationships are supposed to help connect men and women spiritually, sexually, and physically. It helps people to discover their compatibility with a member of the opposite sex. Because of this, people are able to choose who they can live together with. But due to patriarchal tyranny, historically, men often abuse women emotionally, sexually, verbally, and physically in their power struggle to stamp their dominance on their relationships. Instead of trying to exist in a complimentary relationship with their partner, male chauvinists generally disempowered women in the corrupt practices of sexism and patriarchy. These stances merely result in abusive relationships.

Sexist attitudes and patriarchal customs always favour men with the power of veto over women in the household.

> Levels of education, earnings and asset ownership and age gaps are key in determining bargaining power between men and women within the household. Arguably of equal importance is the threat of domestic violence. While physical and sexual violence and other forms of abuse occur in different domestic environments and in different guises, there is substantial evidence to suggest that such acts are mainly perpetrated by adult men against women and girls. Domestic violence threatens the physical health and emotional well-being of its victims and often forces them to endure subordinate positions and economic insecurity within their households.

> Violence against women and girls crosses the boundaries of race, culture, wealth and religion. Every year, thousands of women are maimed or killed by rejected suitors in many countries. A landmark World Health Organisation multi-country study on women's health and domestic violence

against women reveals that of those interviewed, 37 per cent of women in a Brazilian province, 56 per cent of women in a province in the United Republic of Tanzania, and 62 per cent of women in a province in Bangladesh reported having experienced physical or sexual violence by an intimate partner.

The pattern is broadly similar for industrialized countries. According to another key report from the same organisation, the *World report on violence and health*, studies show that 40 per cent to 70 per cent of female murder victims in Australia, Canada, Israel, South Africa and the United States were killed by their husbands or boyfriends— often within the context of an ongoing abusive relationship. In the United Kingdom, 40 per cent of female homicide victims are killed by their intimate partners.[16]

It is asserted that violent acts against women and girls are underreported. Victims are likely to be reluctant to discuss abusive experiences not only because of embarrassment but through fear. Failure to report perpetual violence may poignantly result in death. Women and girls who report experienced violent events, alas, may also suffer the fate of death in some countries. These are shocking realities. Violent personalities result from the complex interplay between social, cultural, and environmental factors of individuals. This explains why some individuals behave violently towards women and girls in some countries than in others. Factors such as chauvinism, sexism, licentiousness, misogyny, jealousy, inequalities, selfishness, and drugs and alcohol abuse are all related to domestic violence. These issues must be militated against in order to repulse the evil aggression of domestic violence.

---

[16]   *The State of the World's Children*, 2007, 23

Chapter 18

So-Called Honour Killing

Oppression against women and girls takes four forms: social, educational, political, and economic. I've recognised that gender-based inequalities often serve as the driving wedge between the disempowerment of females and the dominance of males. The long-established patterns of violence and injustice against women and girls seem to be so deeply entrenched into the fabric of human societies to the point where even UDHR, CEDAW, and CRC have been futile thus far to halt the scourges of women and girls.

Since 1945, human rights have been established in international law. Unfortunately, women and girls have heretofore and still are denied their right to equality, liberty, justice, and security of person. Millions of women are held in servitude and subjected to inhuman and degrading treatment. Not to mention the pervasive facts of them being discriminated against because of their gender and denied their inherent right to life. Because of gender-based biases, millions of women and girls are killed in preservation of family honour (so-called honour killing).

This homicide is committed by the perpetrators who the victim has allegedly brought dishonour upon—the family or community. The perceived dishonour is often deemed as the transgression of acceptable beliefs, or the suspicion of such behaviour. These include attiring in a manner unacceptable, expressing desire to divorce or prevent an arranged marriage, wanting to marry by own choice, or to indulge in infidelity or miscegenation. In some cultures, it is a dishonourable action of a rape victim to report her experience. 'Admitting to having experienced certain violent events, such as rape, may in some countries result in death. In certain cultures, the preservation of family honour is a traditional motive for killing women who have been raped (so-called "honour killings"),' noted *World report on violence and health.*

It is asserted that more than 20,000 women are suspected to be killed in the name of 'honour' every year in the Middle East and Southwest Asia where this gruesome act is most rampant. The consequences of women being powerless, voiceless, and unequal reverberate terribly across the globe. The vexing problems which confront women and girls are so repugnant and loathsome to our modern world. Much has been said and written in condemnation of the ignoble and inhuman practices against women and girls. But reality adequately substantiates that there yet remains far to go in eliminating the loathsomeness of gender-based injustices, brutalities, and violence from our world. Violations of women's human rights permeated every region of the globe. Perpetual legacies of inequality and disempowerment are very detrimental to women and girls.

Chapter 19

Stop Violence against Women

I've heard some jaw-dropping claims in my life. Among these is the claim that there are women who actually believe that if their partner doesn't beat them, they don't love them. That is quite a freakish belief which is nothing short of ignorance. There is no love in physical violence. Masochistic behaviour should not be confused with the noble sentiments and feelings of love. The contrast between masochism and love is very great. Masochism is rather synonymous with sadism. Therefore, only a masochist would desire to be beaten by her partner. That is not an act of being loved but rather a fulfilment of a freaky fantasy to gain sexual gratification from being cruel to or hurting another person.

Frankly, I cannot honestly see any love whatsoever in any acts where sexual gratification depends on the suffering of physical pain or humiliation. Abuse, in all its forms, carries harmful consequences. Having been born in a culture that values the social status of men over women to the extent where they see their mother and, in a probability, their grandmothers conformed to traditional ideas about the roles of men and women, unfortunately, some young women become inured to domestic violence and household inequalities.

Household gender inequalities foster a permissive context for abusive relationships. A UNICEF study indicates that women who marry at a young age are more likely to believe that it is sometimes acceptable for a husband to beat his wife, and are more likely to experience domestic violence than women who marry at an older age. In Kenya, for example, 36 per cent of women who were married before the age of 18 believe that a man is sometimes justified in beating his wife, compared to 20 per cent of those who were married as adults.[17]

Man's inhumanity to woman has proved to be a force of evil to be reckoned with. Much has been done to be rid of the abhorrent acts against women and girls. Nonetheless, a whole lot more remains to be done in order to protect females from violent men. For what has been accomplished thus far is not enough to assure women's safety in their households. It is sad that even to date, so many people have yet to realise that each of us has something to contribute to the eradication of maltreatment of women and girls. There are, however, a few people who are devoted to the cause. But until the masses of human community come together to work unstintingly for the cause, the scourges of our world will not disappear. It is in consequence of this failure why violence against women has continued unabated throughout the world.

We have, at some point in our lives, heard that the hearts of most women are filled with jealousy about their partners. We have, however, heard very little of the fact that women are also pretty jealous of their independence and freedom as well. It is truism to say that any such woman would not desire to become a victim of immoral acts encompassing from physical assault, harassment, rape, verbal abuse to bullying. Licentiousness has resulted to millions

---

[17]   *The State of the World's Children*, 2007, 23

of women and girls being misanthropic of men and even boys. Sexual perversions of men have caused countless women and girls to develop social phobias and physiological burdens.

Everyone who is concerned or involved with improving women's lives and reducing children's suffering, we must remain steadfast in our efforts to liberate females from the state of inequality. In so doing, we can speed the disappearance of gender discrimination from our world. For this, we need more people to contribute to the greater establishment of women's sanctuary in human societies. The masses of the world can and must combine their strength for the advancement of women's standard of living.

Whether it is manifested in public or in private life, the eradication of violence against women must be achieved. The risks and realities of women experiencing violence are far too great in our civilised world. It is shocking when the perpetrators of violence against females are carried out by a totally depraved stranger. But it is even more deeply shocking to know that the violent acts that are primarily committed against women are predominantly perpetrated by men who are supposed to be their lovers, husband, father, etc. There's ample evidence that women are more likely to be victimized by someone that they are intimate with or a close family member. That is really bad, indeed. In my opinion, to treat a woman poorly and to inflict violent or licentious acts upon her is definitely not an act of a lover but that of a misogynist. Furthermore, no man, no matter who he is, has the moral right to perpetrate acts of abuse and violence against women.

The vulnerability of women has been exposed time and time again by their so-called lovers. Women themselves must help efforts to protect them against their villainous partners. Be it known that women who are victimised by domestic violence must pluck up the courage to step out of their subservient position and play a more influential role in the eradication of violence against them and their children. Victims of violence should not make fear hinder them from reporting the perpetrators to the police. If then, the police fail to protect the victims, this can only be deemed as a lawful contribution to violence against women. The same conclusion can be drawn for other governmental officials who fail to protect and promote women's rights through legislation and financing womanitarian programmes.

Violence and abuse against women and girls are too rampant throughout the world. It is essential that we, the true lovers of womankind, strive tirelessly to stop acts of violation and deprivation of woman's human rights. If the masses continue ignoring the victimisation of women by men of depraved, sexist, or misogynistic character, be it known that violence and mistreatment against women will never cease to increase. We should not allow things to get worse before we try to make it better. That is not the works of the wise and prudent.

Chapter 20

Economic Deprivation against Women

I t is an unaccepted behaviour all over the world to be dishonest for pecuniary gains and favouritism. The practices of dishonesty merely prevent the individual from reaching the unquestionable standard of probity and integrity. Dishonesty is a mental disease. Anyone who suffers from this illness is never free from inflicting injustice upon others. It is in consequence of this why people have always been demanding justice.

Greed and selfishness are obvious incitement to unethical behaviour. The unscrupulous desires of controlling men are no exception. As a form of domestic violence, domineering men often bring great upheaval to the present and future prospect of women. As said earlier, men traditional gain power of veto in their intimate relationship through assets and income. So to stamp dominance in their relationship, control freaks often control forcibly their partner's access to economic resources. This is known as financial or economic abuse. This is done to enforce economic dependency.

Men's inhumanity to women takes many forms, including sexual abuse, emotional abuse, controlling/domineering, intimidation, and economic deprivation. Men's obsession with domestic power often results in physical aggression or assault against the women in their intimate relationship. These obsessive men often pride themselves on keeping control on finance and assets in their relationship. This involves taking forcibly the money that their partner earns, not allowing them access to their own bank accounts, or impede them from getting employed. Even worse, force them to leave their jobs or prevent them from obtaining an education. Economic-abused women generally consign to a life of submissiveness and dependency. In this controlled position, the abusers merely give the abused a scant allowance to buy basic necessities such as food and clothes. Furthermore, the abusers often budget every spending of the abused. Even worse, they don't allow women to handle any financial matters or to gain assets. All in all, control freaks deny women of their independence through economic deprivation.

I've learnt that, like other forms of intimate partner violence (IPV), economic deprivation is underreported. Women who are forced into this dependent and submissive corner of their household often fail to discuss their experience of financial/economic abuse. This is because they are often too scared or too ashamed to reveal this to anyone. My advice to those ladies who are victimised by this gross immorality is that, with doubt, they should pluck up the courage and swallow their pride and seek the necessary help to escape this injustice. Reporting the perpetrators to the police is the best solution. Be it known that the grimness of any forms of abuse will never just suddenly vanish from your relationship. So don't be foolish as to believe that one glorious day control freaks will have a change of heart and set their partner free from enforced economic disadvantages. Nothing of the sort will ever happen.

Abusive relationships are not worthwhile. Anyone who abuses a woman economically, emotionally, sexually, or physically will never treat well their partner. The questions to those women who are victims of abuse are (1) is this the way you want to be treated? And (2) is an abusive relationship what you desire? Only they know the answer.

Chapter 21

Vulnerable to Sexual Abuse: Women and Children

I t is with great sadness I've realised that womankind is in a vulnerable position throughout the world. As a result of this, they are constantly exposed to all manner of physical and psychological mistreatments. Sexual abuse/assaults are everyday occurrence in the lives of women and girls. What kind of world is this! There seems to be no sanctity for womankind. Whether in their homes, schools, workplaces, places of worship, and communities, women and girls are not safe from molestation. Far too many men are apprehended by depravity and subsequently lack concern for the welfare of women and children.

The impacts of gender discrimination are pervasively perilous to females. To this extent, women and girls are oppressed in every region of the world. Gender discrimination merely leads to women and girls being victims of verbal, physical, and sexual abuse.

> Girls and women are frequently victims of physical and sexual violence inside and outside the home. Although such assaults are underreported because of the stigma of the crime, a recent multi-country study by the World Health Organisation revealed that between 15 per cent and 71 per cent of

women had experienced physical or sexual assault
from an intimate partner. Domestic violence is
the most common form of violence perpetrated
against women. During armed conflict, rape and
sexual assault are often used as weapons of war.
When complex emergencies force people to be
displaced from their homes, women and girls are at
increased risk of violence, exploitation and abuse—
sometimes from the very security personnel or
other persons charged with their protection and
safety.[18]

The thoughts of licentiousness will never be entertained by an
individual of the highest integrity. They will always see the moral
repugnance of which it represents. Unfortunately, this world is
pervaded by depraved men who take delight in sexual interaction
with children and raping of women. Paedophiles and perverts
merely hinder women and children from freedom of being raped
and molested. Licentious men should be punished severely for their
acts of perversion against women and children. There is no place
for rapists and paedophiles among civilised people.

Owing to the exclusion of life sentence, I find the lawful
punishment of child molesters very lenient. Such leniency
on offenders will never scare them off from engaging in sexual
activities with children. For the benefit of women and children
safety, policymakers of all nations should implement new draconian
laws to punish more severely all acts of paedophilia and sexual
molestations. Let there be no doubt that this will force those
perverted individuals to accumulate some dignity, decency, and
ethical standards to know that it cannot be right but wrong to seek
sexual gratification from molesting children and raping women.
There is a lack of sanctuary for women and girls in this world. Even
in the military, sexual assaults against women are prevalent. In the

---

[18]   *The State of the World's Children*, 2007, 7

US military for example, an estimated 19,000 sexual assaults take place each year.

It is already bad when women and children are molested by totally depraved strangers. It is even worse when they are molested by those who are supposed to love and care for them. For instance, there are men who actually believe that their partners are obligated to have sex with them whenever and however they please. So wrong are those men who force their partner to copulate with them. Actually it is defined by a dictionary that rape is to force someone to have sex when they do not want to. Therefore, anyone who forces their partner to indulge in undesirable sexual activities is culpable for sexual abuse. And that is definitely a form of domestic abuse.

Minors are too vulnerable to acts of paedophilia—in their community, religious place of worship, home, and school. It is quite sickening to ascertain that countless children have been and still are exposed to incest. Paedophiles are infamous for committing the indecent assault of buggery against boys and molesting girls. That is so sickening. No perverted sexual predator should molest innocent children with impunity. Unfortunately, victims of incest can suffer a lifetime of physiological trauma. Regarding the case of incest, to all parents out there, don't shun your daughters or sons, but give them a listening ear and render protective actions in safeguarding their welfare and well-being against licentiousness. This is courtesy of the reggae singer Queen Ifrica as suggested in her song 'Daddy' ('to all yuh maddas out dere give a listening ear pay attention even if di man a pastor yuh affi mek sure before yuh trust him wid yuh dawta plus him wi even tek yuh son as braata').

People whose sanity is intact with good ethical standards must combine their strengths and bring moral pressure to bear on the conscience of those who harbour sexual orientation for children. It doesn't matter if it involves a blood relative, step relative, friend, or a completely depraved stranger; all children molesters must receive due punishment. In the case of relative and parental incest, child molesters often evade punishment. For the victim, relatives are known to cover up this crime in protection of their family reputation. But in the light of justice, anyone who knows of a case of incest and fails to report it to the necessary authority, in my judgement and no doubt others, are equally culpable for the crime. For the prevalence of justice, whether you're the victim or the parent of the victim, or someone who's concerned, if you know about a case of child molestation, let no one deter you from reporting it to the police. The protection of women and children from sexual predators is a cause that all benevolent people of the highest integrity will espouse.

Chapter 22

Cycle of Gender Discrimination

G ender discrimination has proved to be a life cycle. This grim cycle merely consigns hundreds of millions of women to a lifetime of disadvantages and misery. First, as the less-favourable offspring in many cultures, in particular Asia, girls face the mortal enemies of foeticide and infanticide.

> Gender discrimination begins early. Modern diagnostic tools for pregnancy have made it possible to determine a child's sex in the earliest phase. Where there is a clear economic or cultural preference for sons, the misuse of these techniques can facilitate female foeticide.[19]

Many girls who survive sex-selective foeticide and infanticide, unfortunately, go on to suffer from gender-based disadvantages during the middle years of childhood and adolescence. Although most abuses against girls have been outlawed in most countries, the laws are poorly enforced—resulting similar consequence as where they're not outlawed. Furthermore, despite decades of international effort to eradicate these practices, millions of females have and continue to experience human rights abuses. For example, 'it is

---

[19]   *The State of the World's Children*, 2007, 4

estimated that more than 130 million women and girls alive today
have been subjected to Female genital mutilation/cutting (FGM/C),
involves partial or total removal of, or other injuries to, female
genitalia for cultural, nonmedical reasons. The practice of FGM/C
mainly occurs in countries in sub-Saharan Africa, the Middle East
and North Africa and some parts of South-East Asia. FGM/C
can have grave health consequences, including the failure to heal,
increased susceptibility to HIV infection, childbirth complications,
inflammatory diseases and urinary incontinence. Severe bleeding
and infection can lead to death.'[20]

As the world is still characterized by male domination and
female subordination, innumerable girls often face educational
disadvantages at primary and secondary level.

> For every 100 boys out of school, there are 115
> girls in the same situation. Though the gender gap
> has been closing steadily over the past few decades,
> nearly 1 of every 5 girls who enrols in primary
> school in developing countries does not complete
> a primary education. Missing out on a primary
> education deprives a girl of the opportunity
> to develop to her full potential. Research has
> shown that educated women are less likely to die
> in childbirth and are more likely to send their
> children to school. Evidence indicates that the
> under five mortality rate falls by about half for
> mothers with primary school education.[21]

Subordination of girls' secondary education to marriage is the
traditional stance maintained by many societies.

---

[20]   *The State of the World's Children*, 2007, 4

[21]   *The State of the World's Children*, 2007, 4

Recent UNICEF estimates indicate that an average of only 43 per cent of girls of the appropriate age in the developing world attend secondary school. There are multiple reasons for this: There may simply be no secondary school for girls to attend— many developing countries and donors have traditionally focused on offering universal primary education and neglected to allocate the resources to increase enrolment and attendance in secondary education. A girl's parents may conclude that they cannot afford secondary education or may take the traditional view that marriage should be the limit of her ambitions.[22]

Lack of education often resulted in a troubled adolescence for many young women.

Among the greatest threats to adolescent development are abuse, exploitation and violence, and the lack of vital knowledge about sexual and reproductive health, including HIV/AIDS . . . By 2005, nearly half of the 39 million people living with HIV were women. In parts of Africa and the Caribbean, young women (aged 15–24) are up to six times more likely to be infected than young men their age. Women are at greater risk of contracting HIV than men. One important explanation is physiological—women are at least twice as likely as men to become infected with HIV during sex. The other crucial, and largely reversible, factor is social—gender discrimination denies women the negotiating power they need to reduce their risk of infection. High rates of illiteracy among women prevent them from

---

[22]   *The State of the World's Children*, 2007, 4

knowing about the risks of HIV infection and possible protection strategies. A survey of 24 sub-Saharan African countries reveals that two thirds or more of young women lack comprehensive knowledge of HIV transmission. The dramatic increase in infection among women heightens the risk of infection among children. Infants become infected through their mothers during pregnancy, childbirth or breastfeeding. In 2005, more than 2 million children aged 14 years or younger were living with HIV.[23]

Lack of education merely subordinates women in society—weakening women's bargaining power within households and constraining opportunities for women's economic and political participation. Millions of women are forced to marry young and settle into domesticity. Child marriage and premature parenthood carries serious threats to women.

Child marriage is a long-standing tradition in areas where it is practised, making protest sometimes barely possible. Parents may consent to child marriages out of economic necessity, or because they believe marriage will protect girls from sexual assault and pregnancy outside marriage, extend girls' childbearing years or ensure obedience to their husband's household. Premature pregnancy and motherhood are an inevitable consequence of child marriage. An estimated 14 million adolescents between 15 and 19 give birth each year. Girls under 15 are five times more likely to die during pregnancy and childbirth than women in their twenties. If a mother is under 18, her baby's chance of dying in the first year of life is 60 per

---

[23]   *The State of the World's Children*, 2007, 4–5

cent greater than that of a baby born to a mother older than 19. Even if the child survives, he or she is more likely to suffer from low birth weight, under nutrition and late physical and cognitive development.[24]

Because of lack of respect for the female dignity (every being has an innate right to be valued and receive ethical treatment), they face the risks of sexual abuse, exploitation, and trafficking.

> The younger girls are when they first have sex, the more likely it is that intercourse has been imposed on them. According to a World Health Organisation study, 150 million girls and 73 million boys under the age of 18 experienced forced sexual intercourse or other forms of physical and sexual violence in 2002. The absence of a minimum age for sexual consent and marriage exposes children to partner violence in some countries. An estimated 1.8 million children are involved in commercial sex work. Many are forced into it, whether they are sold into sexual slavery by desperately poor families or abducted and trafficked into brothels or other exploitative environments. Children exploited in the commercial sex industry are subjected to neglect, sexual violence and physical and psychological abuse.[25]

Many women live a substandard existence. Poverty has had a pernicious effect on women's health and motherhood. Maternal mortality is high in the poorer countries.

---

[24]   *The State of the World's Children*, 2007, 4

[25]   *The State of the World's Children*, 2007, 5

It is estimated that each year more than half a million women—roughly one woman every minute—die as a result of pregnancy complications and childbirth. Some 99 per cent of all maternal deaths occur in developing countries, with over 90 per cent of those in Africa and Asia. Two thirds of maternal deaths in 2000 occurred in 13 of the world's poorest countries. The same year, India alone accounted for one quarter of all maternal deaths. One out of every 16 sub-Saharan African women will die as a result of pregnancy or childbirth, compared to just 1 out of every 4,000 in industrialized countries. Moreover, motherless newborns are between 3 and 10 times more likely to die than newborns whose mothers survive. Many of these women's lives could be saved if they had access to basic health care services, including skilled attendants at all births and emergency obstetric care for women who develop complications.[26]

Gender bias places females at a distinct disadvantage from birth into old age.

Elderly women may face double discrimination on the basis of both gender and age. Women tend to live longer than men, may lack control of family resources and can face discrimination from inheritance and property laws. Many older women are plunged into poverty at a time of life when they are very vulnerable. Only a few developing countries have safety nets for older people in the form of non-contributory or means tested pensions. Grandmothers in particular possess a

---

[26]   *The State of the World's Children*, 2007, 5

great deal of knowledge and experience related to all aspects of maternal and child health and care. In many families, they are a mainstay of childcare for working parents. Experience has shown that children's rights are advanced when programmes that seek to benefit children and families also include elderly women.[27]

---

[27] *The State of the World's Children*, 2007, 5

Chapter 23

Help Create a Better World for Children

Since its inception in 1946, as the United Nations International Children's Emergency Fund, and known later as the United Nations Children's Fund (UNICEF) in 1954, the organisation has been rendering its humanitarian service to meet the needs of children and help to bring to fruition a brighter and happier future for them. UNICEF exemplifies the true principles of womanitarianism. Programmes initiated by UNICEF merely focus on providing developmental assistance to children's proper upbringing and the well-being of mothers, especially in developing countries.

The organisation has endeavoured unceasingly for the total welfare of the family. It has provided food for millions of mothers and their children. Along with providing sustenance and nourishment, the organisation has been cultivating assistance in the field of education for children as well. UNICEF knows the importance of *Mens sana in corpore sano*—a sound mind in a healthy body. So in its programmes, UNICEF assures food for the body and food for the mind. Although the help provided so far can by no means be considered to have adequately met their needs, the organisation has made significant contribution to the well-being of mothers and children throughout the world.

There are many other organisations campaigning against human rights abuses against women and girls as well as working daily to meet the needs of the poor and have-nots. Unfortunately, there still remain many problems in dire need of solutions. Despite attempts made to control birth, child survival, and mortality, millions of children are still born in misery and die in sickness. Millions of children die in infancy across the globe. Those that survive, in particular the developing countries, are all too often scourged by disease, illiteracy, and hunger. These scourges deny hundreds of millions of children the opportunities and privileges enjoyed by other children of the world.

The disadvantages and problems correlated with poverty are traditionally associated with rural areas. To escape unemployment in particular, rural dwellers often migrate to urban areas with their children, seeking a better life. 'The day is coming when the majority of the world's children will grow up in cities and towns. Already, half of all people live in urban areas. By mid-century, over two thirds of the global population will call these places home,' noted *The State of the World's Children 2012*.

> This report focuses on the children—more than one billion and counting—who live in urban settings around the world.
>
> Urban areas offer great potential to secure children's rights and accelerate progress towards the Millennium Development Goals (MDGs). Cities attract and generate wealth, jobs and investment, and are therefore associated with economic development. The more urban a country, the more likely it is to have higher incomes and stronger institutions. Children in urban areas are often better off than their rural counterparts thanks to higher standards of health, protection, education and sanitation. But urban advances

have been uneven, and millions of children
in marginalized urban settings confront daily
challenges and deprivations of their rights.

Traditionally, when children's well-being is
assessed, a comparison is drawn between the
indicators for children in rural areas and those in
urban settings. As expected, urban results tend
to be better, whether in terms of the proportion
of children reaching their first or fifth birthday,
going to school or gaining access to improved
sanitation. But these comparisons rest on aggregate
figures in which the hardships endured by poorer
urban children are obscured by the wealth of
communities elsewhere in the city.

Where detailed urban data are available, they
reveal wide disparities in children's rates of
survival, nutritional status and education
resulting from unequal access to services. Such
disaggregated information is hard to find, however,
and for the most part development is pursued,
and resources allocated, on the basis of statistical
averages. One consequence of this is that children
living in informal settlements and impoverished
neighbourhoods are excluded from essential
services and social protection to which they have a
right. This is happening as population growth puts
existing infrastructure and services under strain
and urbanization becomes nearly synonymous with
slum formation. According to the United Nations
Human Settlements Programme (UN-Habitat),
one city dweller in three lives in slum conditions,
lacking security of tenure in overcrowded,
unhygienic places characterized by unemployment,

pollution, traffic, crime, a high cost of living, poor
service coverage and competition over resources.[28]

Grinding poverty exposes millions of children to discrimination,
abuse, exploitation, and premature death. Inadequate living
conditions make it difficult for children to survive and thrive.
'Nearly 8 million children died in 2010 before reaching the age of
5, largely due to pneumonia, diarrhoea and birth complications . . .
High urban child mortality rates tend to be seen in places where
significant concentrations of extreme poverty combine with
inadequate services, as in slums.'[29] This articulates that heads of
state or government and the official delegations of countries have
not yet seized the 'opportunity to endorse the universal goals of
ensuring adequate shelter for all and making human settlements
safer, healthier and more liveable, equitable, sustainable and
productive,' enshrined in the Istanbul Declaration on Human
Settlements, or Habitat Agenda, of 1996.

If all children are to survive and thrive, no child can live in
subhuman condition. Every child must enjoy an adequate standard
of living combined with a safe place to play. We must support
initiatives to secure decent housing, safe drinking water, and
sanitation for poorer children and their families. Only these healthy
and safe environments can support children's full development. The
needs of children and infants must be adequately met. The civil,
social, political, cultural, and economic rights of every child must
be equally guaranteed and safeguarded through the Convention
on the Rights of the Child. No child should be deprived of his
or her rights to survival and protection from abuse, child labour,
exploitation, and discrimination. In order for all children to
develop to their fullest, they must have equal access to health care
and education. The principle of non-discrimination in enshrined
in CRC can help prevent violations of children's human rights.

---

[28]   *The State of The World's Children*, 2012, 1–2

[29]   *The State of The World's Children*, 2012, 14

The convention commits state parties to 'respect and ensure the rights set forth in the present Convention to each child within their jurisdiction without discrimination of any kind, irrespective of the child's or his or her parent's or legal guardian's race, colour, sex, language, religion, political or other opinion, national, ethnic or social origin, property, disability, birth or other status' (Article 2).

It is critical to support advocacy and action on behalf of the world's 2.2 billion, especially the most vulnerable ones. It is truism that 'the rights and well-being of children must be at the heart of the goals and targets that the international community sets for the post-MDG era. Whether worthy targets are set and achieved will depend on many factors—not the least of these being whether development decision-makers heed the evidence and listen seriously to poor or otherwise marginalized children and communities.'[30] Providing the facts, it is only fitting for the individuals to aid actions to improve children's lives.

---

[30]   *The State of the World's Children*, 2014, 16

Chapter 24

Support Initiative for Equality in Education

Problems affecting children in urban and rural settings all over the world does not always go unnoticed by the international community. But the attention attracted by these problems is not always received at the same levels of solutions. And so the improvement of the inadequate living conditions of deprived children often lags behind. This does not help in closing the disparities between the underprivileged and the more privileged children of the world. However, thanks to the UN agencies and the millennium agenda, the gender inequality in primary and secondary education will not go unchallenged.

In 2000, the United Nations launched an initiative known as the United Nations Girls' Education Initiative (UNGEI). Adopted by the UN General Assembly on 13 June 2008, UNGEI gives the following vision on its website (www.ungei.org/whatisungei/index_211.html): 'A world where all girls and boys are empowered through quality education to realize their full potential and contribute to transforming societies where gender equality becomes a reality.' UNGEI also charted a mission 'to assist national governments as they fulfil their responsibilities towards ensuring the right to education and gender equality for all children, girls and boys alike. UNGEI works to improve the quality and availability of girls' education in support of the gender-related Education for All goals, the second Millennium Development Goal (MDG) to achieve universal primary education, and MDG 3 to promote gender equality and empower women. UNGEI is committed to accelerating action on girls' education and revitalizing the broad social mobilization and high-level political action needed to ensure that every girl, as well as every boy, receives a quality education.'

Such initiative to reduce the gender gap in schooling is one for a great cause. If fully supported, not by lip service but through meaningful actions, UNGEI will give girls equal access to all levels of education.

> UNGEI facilitates the coordination of girls' education strategies and interventions at the country level through partnerships with governments, donor countries, non-governmental organisations, civil society, the private sector, communities and families. Other partnerships are also working towards the same objective. In 1999, four international civil society organisations— Oxfam International, Action Aid International, Education International, and the Global March against Child Labour—established the Global Campaign for Education (GCE) to work towards elimination of gender disparities in education by 2015.[31]

These partnerships between UN agencies and those organisations are essential to achieving gender parity in education. Donations and volunteer services of womanitarians also provide the key to eliminate gender disparities in education. The populace must support and contribute to both governmental and non-government initiatives to reduce and eradicate threats to girls' health and safety.

---

[31]   *The State of the World's Children*, 2007, 70

Every threat to young women is a threat to the double dividend of gender equality in a society.

There should be no favouritism towards any children in particular education.

> Ensuring that girls and boys have equal educational opportunities is one of the most important and powerful steps towards combating gender discrimination and advancing children's rights. Every girl and boy is entitled to education, regardless of their social or economic status. Enabling girls to access the intellectual and social benefits of basic education ensures that their rights are protected and fulfilled and greatly enhances the range of life choices available to them as women. Furthermore, girls' education has profound and long-lasting benefits for families and entire communities. Women with some formal education are more likely to delay marriage and childbirth, ensure their children are immunized, be better informed about their own and their children's nutritional requirements and adopt improved birth spacing practices. As a result, their children have higher survival rates and tend to be healthier and better nourished. Moreover, in many countries, each additional year of formal education completed by a mother translates into her children remaining in school up to one half year longer than would otherwise be the case.
>
> Recent trends in girls' education provide grounds for some optimism. Over the past 30 years, for example, gross primary enrolment rates for girls in low-income countries have risen from 52 per cent to over 90 per cent.6 But gender disparities remain,

not only at the primary and secondary levels, but
also in tertiary education, where a mere 5 per cent
to 10 per cent of students in low-income countries
are female.[32]

All UN initiatives, conventions, and organisations that are
symbolic with gender equality and the recognition of human
rights for women and children can make a real difference if fully
espoused by member states. It is, therefore, the duty of the ordinary
concerned individuals to campaign for governmental organs to
fully implement those policies. The inaction of the masses of the
world has made impossible so far the beginning of a new era of
well-being and happiness for all women and children. If humanity
is led to develop a more altruistic and womanitarian attitude like
that of UNICEF, surely, the welfare of the world's children will
improve. Following the footsteps of UNICEF and UNGEI, the
world would see the need to improve children's education and
health. In turn, this will provide a healthy and prosperous life for
the present and all succeeding generations.

---

[32]   *The State of the World's Children*, 2007, 71

Chapter 25

Hopes of Mother and Child

The United Nations represents the fundamental hopes of women and children. The United Nations Development Fund for Women (UNIFEM) (est. 1976), the United Nations Educational, Scientific and Cultural Organisation (UNESCO) (est. 1945), the United Nations Development Group (UNDG) (est. 1997), and UNICEF organisations facilitate the UN efforts to further universal respect for equity, social justice, the rule of law, and human rights. These organisations provide the medium to raise the living standard of women and children and to advance global standards of education. They give direction to the Millennium Development Goals (MDGs) set by the UN Charter.

Strict observances to CEDAW, CRC, UNIFEM, and UNESCO are essential if gender equality is to be strengthened and fundamental human rights of women and children are to be adequately safeguarded. Only through abiding respect for the United Nations Charter can member states promote women's human rights, support women's empowerment and gender equality at the global, regional, and national level.

Gender equality is vital to the empowerment of women and girls. Therefore, it is the duty of womanitarians and feminists to endeavour to ensure that this principle is strengthened throughout the world. Gender equality is a moral force to prevent one gender from trampling upon the rights and interests of the other. Gender discrimination is a force of evil which influence injustice and mistreatment of womankind. The principles of CEDAW can advance women's rights, and MDGs can raise the living standards of women and children throughout the world. However, how could it be possible for this international women's rights instrument to be effective when so many states do not implement its policies? If the solutions to the problems faced by women are not secured by this body of international law, then by what obligations will this goal achieve?

It is upsetting to ascertain that most UN member states seem to stint their support when it comes to securing a better life for women and children. If the bulk of the 193 member states that ratified the Millennium Declaration in 2000 fail to align and identify themselves with all aspects of the United Nations' struggle to assure that every individual has the right to dignity, freedom, equality, a basic standard of living that includes freedom from hunger and violence, and encourages tolerance and solidarity, the declaration will fall short of expectation. There is no easy solution to the problems that confront women. But if all nations pull together, the social and economic conditions of women will exceed far beyond our wildest imagination. If UN member states don't become more zealous in solving the problems affecting humanity, all attempts to do so will prove futile. Come 2020, if the organisation objectives continue to be stifled by the inertia of member states, the same futile conclusion will be drawn from MDGs' attempt to achieve its eight international development goals. The goals are

1. eradicating extreme poverty and hunger,

2. achieving universal primary education,

3. promoting gender equality and empowering women

4. reducing child mortality rates,

5. improving maternal health,

6. combating HIV/AIDS, malaria, and other diseases,

7. ensuring environmental sustainability, and

8. developing a global partnership for development.

The hopes of women only weaken by those who oppose the UN principles of human rights. But history teaches us that we should not easily succumb to despair. We know that the privileged will not surrender, willingly, their privileges to the underprivileged. Similarly, male chauvinists and patriarchal tyrants in government will not struggle for gender equality. Therefore, womanitarians and feminists must work together for the eradication of gender inequality. The untenable doctrine of gender discrimination, being a threat to the hopes and aspirations of women, we must work together against the philosophy of sexism and male chauvinism.

I can honestly say that wherever there is gender-based prejudice, there is a basis for greater endeavour to expand gender equality and raise the living standard of women. The world must come to appreciate and embrace the sentiments held by UNICEF for women and children.

> Women are the primary caregivers for children and thus ultimately shape children's lives. This is especially true in the most traditional, patriarchal societies where roles and responsibilities are strictly delineated by gender. The well-being of women and children is inseparable. What is good

building a safer world for all people. So long as these war penchants exist, disarmament and world peace will remain unattainable.

The barbarous acts of war are the most blatant disregard and contempt for human rights. War is perilous to humanity, especially women and children. In countries embroiled in armed conflict, as said earlier, rape and sexual assault are often used as weapons of war against women and girls. Armed conflicts have deprived millions of children of their inherent right to life. 'Millions of children have been killed, injured, orphaned or separated from their families. Millions more have been deprived of schooling in Iraq, Pakistan and other countries embroiled in armed conflict.'[34] War also left millions of children traumatised.

'Regardless of the different countries and different climate they live in, woman in this world are connected and have the same desire in maintaining world peace and love. Obviously, war is one of the major problems which bring disaster on the life of mankind. In spite of the difference of colour, race and religion between women in this world, they all hate war, because the fruit of war is nothing but disaster. War exterminates their beloved husbands, their brothers and their children. It destroys and eliminates their families. At this hour, and such a tragic and sad period where aggressors have planned a very heavy war upon our lives, we would like to bring this to the attention of all women throughout the world, that it is their duty to voice and express solidarity against such acts,'[35] stated Her Majesty Empress Menen Asfaw in September 1935 to the Woman's World Federation. Empress Menen was the consort of Emperor Haile Selassie I of Ethiopia.

Upon the passing of Empress Menen, His Imperial Majesty said: '. . . During the memorable days of Our companionship We never had differences that needed the intervention of others. As Sarah

---

[34] *The State of the World's Children*, 2012, 42

[35] Memorial for Empress Menen Asfaw's Birthday, 25

was to Abraham, so was she obedient to me. Our wishes were mutual until we were separated by the Almighty. Her assistance for the good of the young, the old and the needy requires no testimony for they are greater than thoughts and words.

We have been extremely pleased to live long enough in the perfect union that enable us to see our offspring, our grandchildren and our great grandchildren. We are thankful to the Almighty for having vouchsafed to us that long and uninterrupted union which is not very common in the world today . . .'[36]

Empress Menen's speech, as a case in point, clearly shows that women throughout the world have been trying for ages to combat men's constant desire to embroil in the disease of war. This brings to our attention that no knowledgeable woman loves war. But because women's rights and desires are not secured from violation in this world, men have failed to erase from their minds the thoughts of war. Until men learn to settle their differences peacefully and prevail upon to respect the rights and desires of women, war will not cease.

War has been an extremely divisive issue in human existence. These are critical times for us to voice our humanitarian opinions against such dastardly acts. The inertia and silence of the voice of the masses have made it easy for aggressors to thrust war upon innocent nations. People of the world must become more eager to combat and stop war penchants from waging armed conflicts. Owing to modern arsenals, a world war in this day and age will destroy and devastate the earth and annihilate and exterminate tens and hundreds of millions of humans as well as other living species. Such war would be nothing less than a nuclear holocaust.

These impeding dangers of war should urge us to militate for disarmament and world peace. And at the same time, we should

---

[36]   Selected Speeches of His Imperial Majesty Haile Selassie I, 650

not forget to fight to advance women's political rights. Given the ruthless and inhumane history of males with power of veto in government, more women should be entrusted with the responsibility to lead their nations.

> Empowering women in the political arena can help change societies. Their involvement in governing bodies, whether local or national, leads to policies and legislation that focus on women, children and families. In a survey of 187 women who hold public office in 65 countries, the Inter-Parliamentary Union found that about nine-tenths believe they have a responsibility to represent women's interests and advocate for other members of society.
>
> Women can play key roles in securing peace. Female representation in peace negotiations and post-conflict reconstruction is vital to ensuring the safety and protection of children and other vulnerable populations. Women's direct influence on politics and public policy bodes well for peace, security and prosperity.[37]

These are the facts and not bias claims for matriarchy.

From a humanitarian point of view, there is only one 'just war'. And this is a war on poverty, illiteracy, injustice, disease, and discrimination. In like manner, to enforce the most stringent laws in bringing all human rights abusers to justice. Depraved people will not support any measure taken in militating against acts that are harmful to the interests of humanity.

---

[37] *The State of the World's Children*, 2007, 13–15

Chapter 27

Protect Children against Crime and Violence

H umans are all products of their environment. Evidence shows that no one is a born criminal. Criminality normally interlinks with social and economic disadvantages. Peer pressure is also among the cause of crime and violence. The Chicago School, emerged during the 1920s and 1930s, was the first major field study in urban sociology and later criminology to assert that human behaviour is determined by social structures and physical environmental factors rather than genetic and personal characteristics. Human beings naturally adapt to their environments, which shape their behaviour as individuals or groups. Criminals are generally driven by poverty, greed, and selfishness. These come with terrible price to human communities.

Children who are at the greatest risk of internalising criminal tendencies are those who face the greatest violations of their rights. The most deprived and poverty-stricken children are also the most vulnerable to crime and violence. Poverty is the most obvious and direct cause of crime and violence. CEDAW and CRC are pushed out of reach of countless children because they are poor. Hundreds of millions of children are affected by crime and violence, especially in urban slums. Children are beset by crime and violence in many harmful ways. Some fall victims to the callousness and others participate in the amoral acts. On the other hand, some are witnesses to callous events such as murder, mugging, conflict, and domestic violence. Children who are exposed to crime and violence often suffer psychological problems such as anxiety, depression, and aggression.

Destitution and its harmful consequences impede children's development. It leaves millions of parents and their children struggling to subsist in the squalor of their societies—ghettos, shanty towns, and slums the world over. The cost of education itself is too expensive for the have-nots. Although public schools are plentiful and education is free in many countries, destitute parents simply can't afford to purchase uniforms, educational tools, or pay exam fees for their children. As the inevitable, millions of poor children simply don't attend school or end up being dropouts. Many of these children are forced to work in order to survive. 'Around the world, an estimated 215 million boys and girls aged 5–17 were engaged in child labour in 2008, 115 million of them in hazardous work.' [38]

Children from impoverished neighbourhoods are also prone to join gangs—becoming hoodlums, thugs, or gangsters. The gang culture only exposes young people to a life of criminality. This is one of the direct disadvantages of social and economic barriers. With little hopes and choices because of lack of economic opportunities, millions of desperate and frustrated young people turn to criminal organisations, committing crimes such as armed robbery, extortion, racketeering, petty theft, murder, selling or trafficking drugs, and carjacking. Crime and violence have resulted in premature deaths and incarceration of millions of youths. Many of these young men are fathers, leaving behind the double burden for the mothers of their children to shoulder. To do this, most single mothers work full-time to provide the basic necessities for their children. This leaves them with little, if any, time to physically care for their

---

[38]   *The State of the World's Children*, 2012, 32

children. Lack of parental support and guidance are harmful to the proper upbringing of children.

The disadvantages of poverty predispose children to disease, illiteracy, crime, violence, and the deprivation of their human rights. In order for children to escape the cycle of deprivation and destitution, civil society, local and national governments must support poverty-stricken families to overcome their difficulties. It is a meaningful opportunity for UN states to implement Article 6 of the Convention on the Rights of the Child: 'States Parties recognise that every child has the inherent right to life' and 'ensure to the maximum extent possible the survival and development of the child'. Article 3 is also a good augury to prevent inconsiderateness of the rights of children: 'In all actions concerning children, whether undertaken by public or private social welfare institutions, courts of law, administrative authorities or legislative bodies, the best interests of the child shall be a primary consideration.'

Under the Habitat Agenda, governments also have an obligation to protect the poorest and most vulnerable children and families, especially those in urban slums, to realise their rights to 'adequate shelter for all' and 'sustainable human settlements development in an urbanizing world,' as enshrined in the Declaration on Human Settlements. It has been over fifteen years since the UN-Habitat's Safer Cities Programme was launched in 1996, to tackle urban violence at a local level, especially in Africa, through the development of 'prevention strategies'. But the state of the world's urban children has not changed.

High rates of crime and violence still exist in places where severe insufficiency is an issue—as in urban slums.

> The causes of violence affecting children in urban areas are many and complex, but prominent among them are poverty and inequality. The insufficient provision of public services and such community

vulnerable to human rights violations. This is a violation of Article 7 of CRC: the child has 'the right to know'.

To the downtrodden masses of the world, the international human rights instruments are of relatively unknown quantities. People who are unaware of the Conventions of Human Rights are those who face the greatest violations of their natural and legal rights. This requires particular attention of world leaders to ensure that everyone is enlightened about their human rights in order to stand up and secure their entitlements. UN state parties should act to make sure every citizen of their countries know that 'the term "discrimination against women" . . . mean any distinction, exclusion or restriction made on the basis of sex which has the effect or purpose of impairing or nullifying the recognition, enjoyment or exercise by women, irrespective of their marital status, on a basis of equality of men and women, of human rights and fundamental freedoms in the political, economic, social, cultural, civil or any other field,' as enshrined in Article 1 of CEDAW.

CRC should be taught to every child at primary level. Adults themselves should take priority in becoming knowledgeable of the details of their regional human rights and the international human rights instruments recognised by the UN Assembly. In doing so, the individuals will know when they're being deprived of what they are legally entitled to such as their civil, political, social, cultural, and economic rights. This may also help to prevent the individuals from encroaching upon the rights of others.

It is the duty of governments and policymakers to ensure that all human rights laws are accessible, intelligible, and clear. This fact was recognised by the former British Master of the Rolls, Lord Chief Justice, and Senior Law Lord, Thomas Bingham, when he stated, 'Most obviously, if you and I are liable to be prosecuted, fined and perhaps imprisoned for doing or failing to do something, we ought to be able, without undue difficulty, to find out what it is we must or must not do on pain of criminal penalty . . . bank robbers historically consult their solicitors before robbing a branch of the NatWest, but . . . many crimes are a great deal less obvious than robbery, and most of us are keen to keep on the right side of the law if we can. One important function of the criminal law is to discourage criminal behaviour, and we cannot be discouraged if we do not know, and cannot reasonably easily discover, what it is we should not do . . . If we are to claim the rights which the civil (that is, non-criminal) law gives us, or to perform the obligations which it imposes on us, it is important to know what our rights or obligations are. Otherwise we cannot claim the rights or perform the obligations. It is not much use being entitled to, for example, a winter fuel allowance if you cannot reasonably easily discover your entitlement, and how you set about claiming it. Equally, you can only perform a duty to recycle different kinds of rubbish in different bags if you know what you are meant to do.[40]

---

[40]   *The Rule of Law*, 37–8

Chapter 29

Principles and Values of Respect

The principles and values of respect are essential to establish perfect amity between people. Individuals must pledge their adherence to these ideals in order to behave respectably. Like men, women possess not only virtues but weaknesses. No one is perfect! However, the individuals can strive for perfection by learning from the mistakes and moral precedence set by others as well as those of their own. Also, consider carefully the consequences of one's actions to eliminate regrettable mistakes from future conducts. This will definitely strengthen the individual moral faculty to reach the state of being acumen. In like manner, the adherence to the principle of respectable behaviour must be strictly observed if immorality is to be avoided. We must guard ourselves against insidious activities. We must be vigilant to avoid what is called carelessness, regret, bigotry, intolerance, callousness, malevolence, selfishness . . . the amoral list goes on.

There are many people who're not eager to respect the legitimate rights, beliefs, and interests of others but only those of their own. As a result, the individual's views and opinions about others are often very disrespectful. Those who have failed to broaden their views and knowledge are adjudged to be sacrilegious, self-righteous, bigoted, sexist, racist, etc. It is axiomatic that total respect among people must be accorded in all aspects of life. Any attempt to violate any single aspect will inevitably create dissension and acrimony between the disrespectable and the disrespected.

Respect generates respect, understanding, amity, tolerance, benevolence, and goodwill. But disrespect incites disrespect, violence, argument, conflict, maliciousness, and enmity. No one should denigrate others just because they have different religions or of different genders from themselves. This fact, too, we must recognise. We must treat others with respect and dignity. Respect demands regard for the human rights of all people, without discrimination of any kind, irrespective of their age, race, sex, religion, nationality, ethnic or social origin, etc. One of the core principles of respect is to have consideration for the rights of others. The individuals must also respect their environment and Mother Earth on a whole.

Self-respect cultivates decency. Women, since your gender has been made easy targets to fit the stereotypes of negativity, the individuals should adhere to the true ideal of self-respect. As one example, if a man lives a sexually promiscuous lifestyle, he will be dubbed a player, stud, etc. Thus, he will be simply revered. On the other hand, if a woman was to live the same lifestyle, she would be degraded as a whore, harlot, or bitch. Take it from a man's perspective, men respect and admire a decent lady. Very few men will truly love and respect a woman that indulges in sexual promiscuousness. It is a common adage amongst men that 'you can't turn a whore (or hoe) into a wife'. In others words, men may find women of such sexual habits sexually attractive but not to be their wives. From such women, no doubt, men will seek only sexual gratifications. All women who respect and value themselves positively will abstain from prostituting their dignity and self-worth. Self-respected women are strict observers of abstinence from whoredom, debauchery, and all acts that are an abomination to the ethical standard of decency.

Respect is not a simple word devoid of moral significance, nonetheless. It is an uncompromising principle that demand respect for self and, at the same time, equal respect for others. One cannot disrespect someone and expect that same person to respect him/her. Neither can one be foolish as to behave like the devil's servant and expect to be revered as the Lord's angel. The art of respect lies in the admirable behaviour to make people want to respect the individuals while they are really under no obligation to do so. Respectable people are those who raise the standards by which they judge themselves and by which they are willing to be judged. They, therefore, attire and conduct themselves in accordance with the way they want others to see and treat them.

Don't just stand on your dignity, act to earn your respect. The individuals must be prepared and contented to let people judge the morality of their actions. It is the duty of each individual to adhere to the principles which are designed to exemplify the dignity of one's character. Respect is something that one earns by acting laudably and not something to be demanded by violent force. Respect should not be confused with fear. As one example, there are many abusive men who actually believe their oppressed and mistreated partner respect them. To the contrary, women are more likely to suffer from the social anxiety disorder (SAD or SAnD) of androphobia rather than be respectful of those who abuse them sexually, physically, or verbally. Also, girls who witness or experience those abuses can easily develop the social phobia of intense fear of men.

The traumatic events of rape/sexual assault, physical and verbal abuse have made many women harbour enmity towards men in general. Female mistrust of men normally remains with the sufferers long after being abused. As a direct result, the victims of those licentious crimes tend to become misanthropically hateful of men, even those who did not abuse them. In point of fact, disrespectful, cynical, and immoral behaviour are all incitements to misandry and misogyny in social structures. The principle of respect is indispensible to human development of fondness, love, and admiration of each other. It is well known that love justifies the individual's profound tender, passionate feelings of affection for another person. Naturally in need of this warm affection, humans generally crave the love of each other. Unfortunately, many people have failed to realise that love must be merged with respect in order to fortify and complete the social structure of esteem and admiration among people.

Being loved by someone doesn't necessarily mean that person respects you. Bear in mind that someone can love another but, at the same time, lack respect for that person. But on the other hand, it is rare and recondite for someone to respect another and hate that person at the same time. Love is simply a sense of affectionate feeling. Love is a compulsory instinct of humans. Thus, one can easily develop this feeling for another simply because he or she is a parent, child, relative, or sibling. But no one can just simply respect someone else because of some kinship. Respect, as a condition of being esteemed or honoured, is more demanding than love. Unlike love, respect must always be earned by the individuals through the manifestation of a personal quality or ability. It is good to be loved, but it is more important to be held in respect. Self-respect is fundamental to every dignity of oneself because without it, one cannot be respected by anyone else. Be respectful, and you will be loved and respected!

Chapter 30

Self-Worth

The path to discover the individual's true purpose and identity is already paved with physical and mental growth, personal experiences, and changing social and financial situations. Therefore, the individuals cannot take too much into consideration other people's preconceived opinions about them. Individuals must also refrain from negative evaluation of oneself to the point where it lowers the self-esteem. This is destructive to self-worth. Today, we must look to ourselves to understand our true usefulness and value. We cannot search merely for our positives but negatives as well. In facing the facts of our flaws, we may not be able to take comfort but, at least, encouragement from the enlightenment to convert our weaknesses into strengths and negatives into positives. It is impossible for anyone to give self-approval of his or her worthiness without self-confidence. To be courageous, the individuals must develop self-confidence.

A high self-esteem is essential to self-worth. Far too many individuals lower their self-esteem trying to match up to society's concept of worth in terms of ability, achievements, status, appearances, etc. Because of moral weakness, many individuals evaluate themselves negatively, as their socio-economic status, image, and physical and mental attributes do not measure up to society's acceptance. In consequence, this leads many down the path of self-destruction. For lack of personal worth and self-respect can have a dangerous impact on individuals. Among these are low self-esteem, self-hatred, self-doubt, self-harm, and drugs and alcohol abuse.

People without self-worth are also vulnerable to the perils of peer pressure. To resist temptations to indulge in the immoralities and debaucheries to be accepted by others are true exemplification of self-worth of the highest degree. Immoral persuasion of others should not divert us from our moral self-perception. As we know, everyone has a mind of their own. So we all think differently. Human minds entertain both good and evil thoughts. We must be extra vigilant to avoid accepting the evil or negative thoughts of others. You have a mind of your own. So use it promptly and thoroughly to filter information in order to accept only good influences.

The individuals who administer themselves in accordance with the high standard of self-discipline will, undoubtedly, glow with self-worth and dignity. Every knowledgeable person knows that humans are characterised not only by physical beauty but moral beauty as well. But many people actually believe that physical attraction is the mere essence of beauty. That is inaccurate. For if an Adonis abuses his partner, such a handsome and attractive young man is an individual of an ugly character. And if a gorgeously svelte woman takes delight in sexual promiscuousness, then she's also an individual of an ugly character. Beauty also prevails in moral forms. Therefore, a person may not be the most attractive in terms of physical appearance but exhibits or models more moral beauty than those who are. What is more beautiful, moral or physical attraction? In my judgement, the answer is good morality.

Young girls in particular must conduct themselves decently. This will certainly keep intact their dignity and self-respect. This principle all women must adhere to even if it involves the improvement of their womanliness. Take it from a man's perspective, the quality of being womanly is an omen of respect and admiration. Young girls in particular must be steadfast in decency in order to glow with the highest dignity and esteem. When individuals avoid indecent lifestyles, they actually set themselves up as good role models. No one should be as foolish as to allow others to undermine their self-worth and dignity. Anyone who does so will take no pride in the existence of who they really are.

Chapter 31

Values of Being Mutual

Perfect amity only exists in relations where the principles of being mutual are practised in all aspects. Unless this foundation is established, the feelings and favours between people will lack in harmony, honesty, sincerity, and trust. The morally intact people that we hold in great affection, undoubtedly, will harbour great feelings of affection for us. We must give due consideration to this basic truth that reciprocation is the basis for mutual giving and receiving between people. The value of reciprocal respect and understanding are both indispensible to the greater good of human relations. Only such principle provides the medium whereby people behave in the same manner or agree to help and give each other advantages. Mutuality is the ultimate guide to stimulate healthy interpersonal relationships.

Being mutual is the most fundamental prerequisite to the establishment of any meaningful and productive relationship. The state of being unequal does not yield the balance exchange of feelings or obligations between people. If the individuals wish to receive an equal return, an interchange of some kind between themselves and others, they must act just. It is through *reciprocal favours and feelings* that humans are able to establish lasting relationships. If a man is philogynous towards his partner, she is more than likely to denote her philandry of fondness, love, or

111

admiration for him. But if he mistreats or shows her hatred, she may well disdain him. The foundation and essential characteristics of a healthy relationship are mutual trust and esteem. Unless the individuals undertake a just approach to life and subsequently behave reciprocally with others, their striving desire for good and lasting relations becomes unattainable. People who don't understand the true value of being mutual generally fall victim to temporary contentment and petty satisfactions of being unfair towards others.

Mutuality is very purposeful and worthwhile. This state of being helps prevent people from harbouring disregard and contempt for the human rights of others. The prosperity of our relationships depends on our willingness to take into consideration the welfare and well-being of each other. Acts of selfishness will definitely decrease mutuality and, in turn, increase arguments and disagreements between people. Just as a society that is not just cannot be free of hostility and enmity, so is a relationship. It cannot be denied that if the individuals' pursuit of life limits them to take delight in satisfying their selfish desires, they will subordinate the rights and interests of others. Unfairness, in all its forms, is an incitement to hatred and belligerent relation between people. *Equality* in respect and love are vital ingredients to balance favours and feelings between people.

Man must live in complimentary relationship with woman, treating each other equally with respect and affection. Both male and female chauvinism are poisons of hatred and discriminatory behaviour. Sexism and inequalities inevitably erode interpersonal relationships. Let's adhere to the principles that are basically mutual. Individuals must treat others in the same regards as befits the treatment which they demand for themselves. Our behaviour as dignified people must be to establish relationships which are devoid of hostility and acrimony. To avoid this, we must deal with each other on the basis of mutuality and equality.

Chapter 32

Gender Roles Facts

Men have composed a lot of myths about women to support their sexist stance. To accept misinformation as gospel will only hinder the individual from learning the truth. It is simply a moral weakness to be indoctrinated into vice ideologies. Chauvinistic ideologies that hold men superior and women inferior are, in fact, extremely inaccurate. But men have achieved social, political, and economic success in incorporating these misconceptions into society. Men have, for many centuries, brought their partial influences to bear heavily upon women to secure the most privileged positions in all areas of society. Through the implementation of male supremacy, women have had to bear the stamp of inferiority. In defiance of this bias, men have contributed immeasurably to the mistreatment of women.

Role plays in society is at the core of social inequality and economic injustice practices against women. In the human community, the status of individuals has come to be measured by their possessions. Being aware of this, society gave partial priority to the prospects of men and restricting those of women. Employment, especially professional jobs, became a source of power, prestige, high income, high socio-economic status, and privileges in social and interpersonal relationship. This view is generally dictated by gender-based differentiation between what is considered appropriate roles for men or women in the workplace and in interpersonal relationships. But in view of history, I can honestly say the roles that are generally considered appropriate for woman are often too partial.

Gender roles vary considerably between cultures across the globe. These roles are normally determined by perceived biological and physiological differences. But the concept of gender roles is a historic weapon of patriarchal cultural traditions—used in empowering men and disempowering women. Society generally manipulates women from very early on in life to allow men to dominate its social environment. Male supremacy is a product of socialisation. Most cultures actually teach boys very early on in life to categorise themselves as the patriarch in their social and interpersonal relationships. As a result, society mostly demands more of girls than boys in household labour.

> Gender is a crucial determinant of whether a child engages in labour. While child labour is an infringement of the rights of all children—boys and girls alike—girls often start working at an earlier age than boys, especially in the rural areas where most working children are found. Girls also tend to do more work in the home than boys. As a result of adherence to traditional gender roles, many girls are denied their right to an education or may suffer the triple burden of housework, schoolwork and work outside the home, paid or unpaid. [41]

Most societies have their own myths about women. There are even menstruation myths among these. But men commonly believed every false idea about women. And so, credulous men fail to discover the truths about women. Gender roles, for example, are

---

[41]   *The State of the World's Children*, 2007, 48

sets of social and behavioural norms created supposedly to help humans distinguish what is appropriate for men or women. It is a male chauvinistic myth that women are inherently suitable for subordinated gender roles. Evidence exposed the myth that gender roles are not inborn. Instead, they're rather taught and imposed.

Stereotypes and biases generally form the basis of gender-based differentiation that kept women and girls socially and economically disadvantaged. Male supremacists often undermine women with inequality of gender roles. Within the household, for example, gender roles are generally inequitable and unjust towards women and girls. Cultural attitudes of gender roles towards females within families, unfortunately, are most likely to position them to do the bulk of the labour within the household. Gender roles also deny women decision-making positions within the household. These inequities are deeply entrenched in most societies.

As with most things in life, there is a balance to be struck in roles of male and female. Gender roles, therefore, can only be considered appropriate if it acts as an impartial scale that balances equally the morals and duties of women and men, boys and girls. Every act of inequality is inappropriate. De jure equality of opportunity and treatment of women can accelerate. There must be an adequate safeguard of fairness in human rights to advance equality.

This can be achieved. That is if UN state parties 'take all appropriate measures to modify the social and cultural patterns of conduct of men and women, with a view to achieving the elimination of prejudices and customary and all other practices which are based on the idea of the inferiority or the superiority of either of the sexes or on stereotyped roles for men and women. To ensure that family education includes a proper understanding of maternity as a social function and the recognition of the common responsibility of men and women in the upbringing and development of their children, it being understood that the interest of the children is the primordial consideration in all cases' (Article

5, CEDAW). States parties must also 'take all appropriate measures to eliminate discrimination against women in order to ensure for them equal rights with men in the field of education and . . . the elimination of any stereotyped concept of the roles of men and women at all levels' (Article 10, CEDAW).

Gender role myths are very destructive to the self-actualization, independence, and creativity of women and girls. Gender role myths have and still hinder hundreds of millions of females in their desire to use all their abilities to achieve and be everything that they possibly can. Male chauvinism is a major part of and a partial justification for the subordination and oppression of women. It is of great importance for humanity to grasp with the ultimate fact that all people are equally important and should have the same rights and opportunities in life. Society's principles must be basically egalitarian for the achievement of everyone's full potential.

Chapter 33

Woman's Recognitions

By now, the world should accept that women are, by no means, less than men. Civilisation in its magnitude must be able to foster tolerance, equality, and goodwill. Without the women of the world, undoubtedly, no aspect of human existence is possible. Like men, the roles of women sustain humanity. Gender is not a pretext for superiority or inferiority but a guiding principle to distinguish between man and woman, between boys and girls. Being a man does not necessarily mean one can play a better role in society than that of a woman or vice versa.

Inasmuch as how men act as if their achievements alone contributed to the advancement of civilisation. In fact, women have also made pivotal contributions to human progress. It is cognisable that many men have succeeded at the expense of subordinated women. If they were allowed, many women would have outshone their male counterparts. In Jamaican folklore where there is no stricture on women, for example, Louise Bennett-Coverley (1919–2006), better known affectionately as Miss Lou, is indisputably the island's greatest poet and folklorist ever. Additionally, Jamaica is renowned for its reggae music through singers such as Jimmy Cliff, Bob Marley, Peter Tosh, and Grace Jones . . . the list goes on. These singers were once signed to Island Records. However, Millie Small became Jamaica's first superstar in 1964 with her cover version of

hatred and ignorance towards women. But only a corrupted mind will not find it in his heart to be able to endeavour for the greater good of womankind. But those with the mental attitude of egalitarianism will strive towards the goal of total equality for all humans without any regards. It is of no less importance to someone of the sort to recognise the contributions that women have made and can make to the advancement of civilisation. Henceforth, we must not only labour to assure that women live in peace, equality, and well-being but also honour the names and achievements of them as well. It is only fitting to show special respect, love, and appreciation towards women on International Women's Day (8 March every year) in celebration for women's economic, political, and social achievements.

Chapter 34

Professional Nursing

One of the things that attract my admirations readily is the health care profession of nursing. I entertain nothing but the utmost respect for those nurses in their specialised field to render such great humanitarian deeds to care for the individuals, families, and communities so they may attain, maintain, or recover their health and well-being. It is noble of those nurses who help their fellow being that are bedevilled by pain and scourged by disease. It is a mark of great discipline by those who pursue their ambition as to study and received the credentials and qualifications for this noble profession.

The infants, mothers, the elderly, the disabled, and the sick all enjoy the fruits of the labour of professional nursing. Society on a whole reaps the benefits of the profession. In fact, the seed of professional nursing was sown by a woman. The English nurse Florence Nightingale is credited with planting this noble seed, which has grown into a great tree with many thriving branches within the health care. Nightingale came to prominence in the Crimean War (October 1853–February 1856), which was fought between the Russian Empire and an alliance of the French Empire, the British Empire, the Ottoman Empire, and the Kingdom of Sardinia.

During the yearly stage of the war, medical conditions were said to be far from hygienic or ideal. As a result, mortality rate and fatal infections were high among wounded soldiers. When news of the horrific conditions reached Britain, the secretary of state for war, Sidney Herbert, approached Nightingale to go to the Ottoman Empire to give solution to the medical issues affecting the wounded. Nightingale, along with her team of women volunteer nurses that she trained, arrived at Scutari Barracks (modern-day Üsküdar in Istanbul), Turkey, in November 1854.

It is asserted that even in her early days at the army barracks, the soldiers continued to suffer heavy casualties from typhoid, typhus, dysentery, and cholera than battle wounds. During her first winter at Scutari, 4,077 soldiers died there. But Nightingale eventually reduced the death rate from 42 per cent to 2 per cent. This is said to be achieved either by Nightingale's improvements in hygiene or by calling for the Sanitary Commission to support sick and wounded soldiers of the British Army. Because of her selflessness to tend to patients even at night, she was dubbed by the soldiers as the Lady with the Lamp.

But there is no lack of critics about Nightingale. They claimed that 'the death toll at Nightingale's hospital was higher than at any other hospital in the East'. They put this down to lack of knowledge on her path to deal with the unsanitary conditions at Scutari. But what is undisputed, though, is her selflessness and altruism. As a mark of a sagacious person, Nightingale did not view her experience at Scutari negatively but one that taught her some valuable lessons in nursing, which she later taught the world.

After serving in the war, she returned to England in 1856. In her burning desire to help the sick, the Lady with the Lamp laid the first cornerstone of professional nursing when she established the first secular school for training nurses at St Thomas' Hospital in London in 1860. To solidify her philosophy of nursing, Nightingale published her book the *Notes on Nursing* in 1859. Therein, Florence

Nightingale made a significant attempt in revamping the practice of treating others, including sanitation, military nursing, and hospital practices. Many of her contributions to nursing are still in practice today while others have been modernised.

Mother Seacole

The Jamaican nurse, Mary Jane Seacole (1805–1881), is another woman that came to prominence in the Crimean War. Although both Seacole and Nightingale have gained widespread acknowledgement, Seacole has had to journey a tougher road to the Ottoman Empire. Mary Seacole, seeking to volunteer her service to the British Army, travelled from Navy Bay, in Panama, to England in 1854. She then went on rigmarole from the war office to the quartermaster general and then the medical department. But Seacole was refused at every turn. Seacole was met with rebuff because of her ethnicity. For at that time, people of African descent were overtly confronted by racial discrimination in Britain and elsewhere.

Seacole also applied to no avail to the Crimean Fund (fund raised by public subscription to support the wounded in Crimea) for sponsorship to travel to Crimea. After all those rejections, the undeterred and determine Seacole eventually funded her own journey to the Crimean peninsula. There she established the British Hotel near Balaclava. Built from salvaged materials, the hotel was opened in March 1855 to provide 'a mess-table and comfortable quarters for sick and convalescent officers'. At a total cost of £800, Seacole's hotel was completed in July the same year.

Combining her knowledge of traditional Jamaican herbal medicine with European medical practices, Mary Seacole's hotel was an effective medical centre for the wounded. She also travelled to the battlefield, sometimes under fire, to render her services to wounded soldiers. On one unfortunate day, Seacole dislocated her right thumb while she was attending to wounded soldiers under fire.

Chapter 35

Inventions by Women

Many thoughtless and unknowledgeable people actually believe that the advanced development of this world is solely achieved by men. And so, they literally translate the gender-neutral word *manmade* as a male invention or accomplishment. To the contrary, women have and still are contributing to the advancement of life's comforts. Many noteworthy developments in the field of inventions have been assured by many great women. Despite the historical suppression of women, the recorded inventions of women give ample evidence of how industrious and resourceful they really are. I feel proud to observe the ingenuity of women. The ingenuity of our foremothers bespeaks the greatness of those inventors of the precious feminine gender. Like men, women have provided humanity with tools to reduce the burdens of our tasks and increase our comfort, welfare, well-being, and prosperity.

It is only fitting for the present and future generations to revere the names of our foremothers who, through their courage, wisdom, and foresight, devoted their lives to the greatness and advancement of human civilisation. The biography of those noble women should be taught in schools to honour each one of them. This will not only help to preserve their names but also cause the past to become inspirational to encourage present and future generation of females to accomplish greater things with stronger zeal and devotion by reminding them of the greatness of their foremothers. It is attested that past greatness is not only a source of gratification but a foundation of inspiration of future achievements.

We must keep alive the vivid memories and be appreciative of the inventions of those ingenious women. Many of our foremothers have overcome tremendous odds to blaze the trial in human progress in the field of inventions. Although confronted by sexism, racism, and hardship, women inventors have prevailed significantly over those obstacles. Women of African descent in the United States of America, for example, have had to bear the 'triple oppression'—classism, racism, and sexism. In spite of those social and economic barriers, Afro-American women had pioneered some remarkable inventions. Sarah E. Goode, for instance, was born into slavery in 1850. After freedom, she became an entrepreneur and inventor. Goode's most notable invention is a folding cabinet bed. She received a patent for it on 14 July 1885, as the very first African American woman to receive a United States patent.

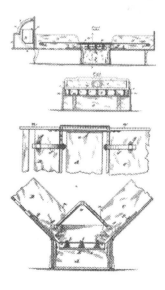

Goode's cabinet bed.

The schoolteacher, Miriam Benjamin, was the second African American woman to receive a patent in 1888. Benjamin received a patent for her invention of the Gong and Signal Chair for hotels. This invention allowed hotel attendants to signal waiters of wanted service by the press of a button on the back of the chair. Benjamin's invention was such a great success to the point where it was used in the United States House of Representatives.

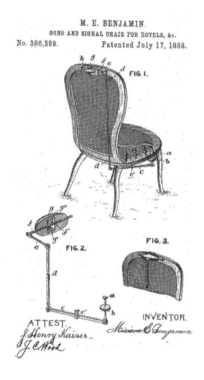

Benjamin's patent for the Gong and Signal Chair for Hotels.

Dr Patricia Bath is another pioneering female inventor. Dr Bath is a 1968 Howard University School of Medicine doctoral degree graduate. She was the first African American female doctor (ophthalmologist) to patent a medical invention. Bath received a patent in 1988 for her invention of the Laserphaco Probe, a laser device that improves the method of removing cataracts.

The following is a list of other women inventors:

Invention	Inventor	Year
disposable cell phone	Randice-Lisa Altschul	1999
signal generators	Dr Betsy Ancker-Johnson	1966
windshield wiper	Mary Anderson	1905
Newborn Scoring System (also called the Apgar Score), for assessing the health of newborn infants	Virginia Apgar	1949
'Method of Obtaining Intensified Image from Developed Photographic Films and Plates.'	Barbara Askins	1978
A fireproof building material called Geobond	Patricia Billings	1997
'Film Structure and Method of Preparation' or invisible, non-reflective glass	Katherine Blodgett	1938
A device to help disabled people eat with less difficulty	Bessie Blount	1951
Improvement to the ironing board	Sarah Boone	1892
Nystatin, the world's first useful antifungal antibiotic	Elizabeth Lee Hazen and Rachel Fuller Brown	1957
dishwasher	Josephine Garis Cochran	1893
A pyrotechnic signalling system known as maritime signal flares	Martha J. Coston	1871

Actar, a mannequin used to teach CPR or cardio pulmonary resuscitation	Dianne Croteau	1989
Discovered radioactive metals i.e. radium & polonium and furthered X-ray technology.	Dr Marie Curie	
The convenient disposable diaper	Marion Donovan	1950
The leukaemia-fighting drug 6-mercaptopurine, drugs that facilitated kidney transplants, and other drugs for the treatment of cancer and leukaemia, development of Imuran, a drug that aids the body in accepting transplanted organs, and Zovirax, a drug used to fight herpes	Gertrude Elion	mid-late 1900s
A petroleum refining method and one of the most inventive chemists of all time	Edith Flanigen	
The home diabetes test	Helen Free	mid 1940s
naturally coloured cotton (FoxFiber)	Sally Fox	1989
Electric food mixer, shelves inside refrigerator doors, and the famous trash can with a foot-pedal lid-opener.	Lillian Moller Gilbreth	
Liquid Paper (originally called mistake out)	Bette Nesmith Graham	mid 1950s

The use of X-ray techniques to find the structural layouts of atoms and to discover the overall molecular shape of over 100 molecules including: penicillin, vitamin B-12, vitamin D, and insulin	Dorothy Crowfoot Hodgkin	
The computerized telephone switching system	Erna Schneider Hoover	1971
modern brassiere (bra)	Mary Phelps Jacob	1913
vacuum-packed canning methods of preserving food	Amanda Theodosia Jones	
permanent wave machine	Marjorie Stewart Joyner	1928
Improved combined sink and washtub design. Later, sloped countertops and glass-doored cabinets, a space saving bed that folded away into the wall, and the K Brick.	Anna Keichline (architect)	1920s
A process for weaving straw with silk or thread	Mary Dixon Kies (the first woman to receive a US patent on 15 May)	1809
Forward Sleeve design	Gabriele Knecht	
A new machine part that automatically fold and glue paper bags to create square bottoms for paper bags.	Margaret Knight	1860s
Rotary engine		1904

First-wave feminism took place during the nineteenth and early twentieth century throughout the world, particularly in the United Kingdom, Canada, the Netherlands, and the United States. It focused on women's suffrage (the right to vote). During the early 1960s and lasting through the late 1990s, second-wave feminism was also a worldwide period of feminist activity, particularly in the United States, Europe, and parts of Asia, such as Turkey and Israel. Second-wave feminist advocacy focused more on a wide range of issues such as sexuality, family, the workplace, reproductive rights, de facto inequalities, and official legal inequalities.

The feminist movement played a pivotal role in women gaining access to medical education and employment in the health professions in many countries. This parity in the medical professions occurred as a result of the repeal of discriminatory laws and abrogation of stereotypical customs directed at women in liberal societies. In the United States of America, for example, because of women's rights movements, in particular the National Organisation for Women (NOW), the US legislators were persuaded to enact *sex* in the Civil Rights Act of 1964, which originally outlawed discrimination against race, colour, religion, and national origin but not gender. In 1967, the Executive Order 11375 was signed by President Lyndon B. Johnson, banning discrimination on the basis of sex in hiring and employment in both the United States federal workforce and on the part of government contractors.

The Executive Order 11375 became a potent weapon for women's rights activists in their fight for employment in universities and colleges in the US. Bernice Sandler pioneered the use of the order in her campaign for employment at the University of Maryland in 1969. Bernice Sandler was instrumental in the enactment of Title IX. As a result, she was called the Godmother of Title IX by the *New York Times*. Title IX of the Education Amendments of 1972 and the Public Health Service Act of 1975 were enacted to prohibit gender discrimination. For instance, Title IX's Equal Opportunity in Education Act states in part that: 'No person in the United States shall, on the basis of sex, be excluded from participation in, be denied the benefits of, or be subjected to discrimination under any education program or activity receiving Federal financial assistance.'

Medical Schools for Women

Although women were given parity in the medical profession, men continued to dominate acceptance into medical schools in many countries. In consequence, females in the medical workforce were and still are disproportionate to the great number of males in many countries. Because of the biases against women, they were systematically denied the opportunity to earn an MD (doctor of medicine, an advanced university degree needed to work as a medical doctor). In many countries where gender partiality was practised, selfless and visionary women had endeavoured to establish medical schools for women. The English physician, teacher, and feminist, Sophia Louisa Jex-Blake (1840–1912), was a pioneer in the establishment of medical schools for women. Jex-Blake was one of the first female doctors in Great Britain and Ireland. Moreover, she was a leading campaigner for medical education for women and was involved in founding the London School of Medicine for Women (est. 1874) and the Edinburgh School of Medicine for Women in Edinburgh, Scotland (est. 1886). The London School of Medicine for Women was the first medical school in Britain to train women.

In addition, there were other schools that were established to train woman physicians. In the United States of America, to begin with, the first medical institution in the world established to train women in medicine and offer them the MD was the Woman's Medical College of Pennsylvania (founded in 1850), also known as MCP. Originally called the Female Medical College of Pennsylvania, the college changed its name to Woman's Medical College of Pennsylvania in 1867. The Saint Petersburg State soldiers and the native inhabitants. She performed the first caesarean section in Africa by a British surgeon in which both the mother and child survived the operation.

- Maria *Lovisa* **Åhrberg** or *Årberg* (1801–1881) was the first recognised woman doctor and surgeon in Sweden.

- Amalia Assur (1803–1889) was the first woman dentist in Sweden and possibly Europe.

- Ann Preston (1813–1872) was the first female to become the dean of a medical school, a position that allowed her to champion the rights of women to become physicians. Preston was also a member of the temperance movement and the Clarkson Anti-Slavery Society.

- Elizabeth Blackwell (1821–1910) was the first woman to receive a medical degree in the United States, as well as the first woman on the UK medical register. She was the first openly identified woman to graduate from medical school, a pioneer in promoting the education of women in medicine in the United States, and a social and moral reformer in both the United States and in England.

- Rebecca Davis Lee Crumpler (1831–1895) was the first African American woman physician in the United States. (Rebecca J. Cole (1846 –1922) was the second, and Susan Maria McKinney Steward (1847–1918) was the third to earn a medical degree and the first in New York state.) Crumpler's publication of *A Book of Medical Discourses* in 1883 was one of the first by an African American about medicine.

- Lucy Hobbs Taylor (1833–1910) was the first woman to graduate from dental school (Ohio College of Dental Surgery in 1866) in the United States.

- Madeleine Brès (1839–1925) was the first woman to have earned a French MD.

- Nadezhda Prokofyevna Suslova (1843–1918) was the first Russian woman to have obtained an MD.

- Elizabeth Garrett Anderson (1836–1917) was a pioneer woman doctor in Britain; she was the co-founder of London School of Medicine for Women (as aforementioned).

- Frances Elizabeth Hoggan (1843–1927) was the first British woman to receive a doctorate in medicine from a university in Europe (1870) and the first female doctor to be registered in Wales.

- Edith Pechey-Phipson (1845–1908) was a pioneer of female doctors in the United States—MD in 1877, University of Bern and Trinity College Dublin. She was one of the first women doctors in the United Kingdom and a campaigner for women's rights. She spent more than twenty years in India as a senior doctor at a women's hospital and was involved in a range of social causes.

- Margaret Cleaves (1848–1917), MD, was a physician, pioneer of electrotherapy and brachytherapy, also known as internal radiotherapy, sealed source radiotherapy, curietherapy, or endocurietherapy. She was also an instructor in Electro-Therapeutics New York Postgraduate Medical School.

- Aletta Henriëtte Jacobs, better known as Aletta Jacobs (1854–1929), was the first woman to complete a university course in the Netherlands and the first Dutch female MD, physician.

- Maria Cuţarida-Crătunescu (1857–1919) was the first Romanian female MD.

- Dolors Aleu (1857–1913) was the first female MD in Spain.

- Anandi Gopal Joshi or Anandibai Joshi (1865–1887) and Kadambini Ganguly (1861–1923) were the first two Indian women to obtain a medical degree through training in Western medicine in 1886.

- Emma K. Willits (1869–1965) was a pioneering woman physician and surgeon who played an important role in the development of the Children's Hospital in San Francisco (now the California campus (Women and Children's Center) of the California Pacific Medical Center), serving as the head of the Department of General Surgery from 1921 to 1934. She is believed to be the third woman to specialize in surgery in the United States.

- Princess Vera Ignatievna Gedroits (1870–1932) was a Russified Lithuanian princess, a doctor of medicine, a professor, the first female surgeon in Russia. She was one of the first female professors of surgery in the world.

- Maria Montessori (1870–1952) was the first female MD in Italy.

- Hannah Myrick (1871–1973) was a physician who received her medical degree from Johns Hopkins University in 1900, thereby helping to blaze the trail for more women to enter medicine. She practised medicine in Boston and acted as the superintendent of the New England Hospital for Women and Children, where she helped to introduce the use of X-rays to treat women and children.

- Yoshioka Yayoi (1871–1959) was one of the first women to gain a medical degree in Japan—founded a medical school for women in 1900, aforementioned.

- Marie Diana Equi (1872–1952) was an American doctor and anarchist.

- Muthulakshmi Reddi (1886–1968) was one of the early women doctors in India. She was a social reformer and founder of a significant medical institution—MD in 1912, Madras Medical College. Dr Reddi was the first woman legislator in India, appointed to the Madras Legislative Council in 1927.

- Chau Lee Sun (1890–1979) was one of the early female Chinese doctors of Western medicine in China. After graduation from Hackett College of Medicine for Women in the late 1910s, she became a staff physician at the David Gregg Hospital for Women and Children in Guangzhou, China.

- Safiye Ali (1891–1952) was the first Turkish woman medical doctor. She treated the soldiers in the Turkish War of Independence (19 May 1919–24 July 1923), the Balkan Wars (1912 and 1913), and in World War I (28 July 1914–11 November 1918). She was educated in Germany in 1916.

- Virginia Apgar (1909–1974) was an American paediatric anaesthesiologist. She was a leader in the fields of anaesthesiology and teratology and effectively founded the field of neonatology. As aforementioned, she is the developer of the Apgar score, the method of assessing the health of newborn babies that has drastically reduced infant mortality throughout the world. Apgar was the first woman granted full professorship at Columbia University College of Physicians and Surgeons.

- Badri Teymourtash (1911–1989) is the first Iranian female dentist, educated in Belgium. In the 1960s she assisted in founding Mashad University's School of Dentistry. During the 1980s the library at Mashad University's School of Dentistry was renamed in her honour.

- Jane Elizabeth Hodgson (1915–2006) was an American obstetrician and gynaecologist. She was an advocator for women's rights.

- Barbara Ross-Lee (b.1942), DO (doctor of osteopathic medicine), was the first African American woman dean of a US medical school (1993, Ohio University College of Osteopathic Medicine).

- Nancy C. Andrews (b.1958) is an American biologist noted for her research on iron homeostasis. She was the first woman dean of a major medical school in the United States (2007, Duke University School of Medicine).

Chapter 38

Women's Contribution to Science

Centuries of women's social, political, economic, and academic subordination and suppression stands as a bias cultural paradigm of man's greed for gender superiority in human societies. This has proven to be women's biggest obstacle in obtaining an education and participation in many fields of science. Women were seen more fitting to settle in domesticity than to enter into the scientific spheres. Science itself was an obstacle that women faced. For science contributed to the widespread theories that women were allegedly mentally and socially inferior to men, best suited to play a minion role in society.

Biases against women have resulted in many countries' failure to give due consideration to their rights and interests. This has led to the centuries of stricture on the involvement of women in the fields of scientific consensus or mainstream science. In the historic philosophy of science, few women are recorded to have contributed to protoscience. In ancient Greece where the study of natural philosophy was open to women, several women are noted for their contribution in alchemy and astrology, which became chemistry and astronomy in modern science from the eighteenth and seventeenth century, respectively. For instance, Aglaonike, also known as Aganice of Thessaly (*fl.* second century BC), is cited as the first female astronomer in ancient Greece. She could predict the

Other recorded phenomenal females involved in contributing to science in the eighteenth century include

- Maria Sibylla Merian (1647–1717) was a naturalist and scientific illustrator who studied plants and insects and made detailed paintings about them. Her detailed observations and documentation of the metamorphosis of the butterfly make her a significant, albeit not well known, contributor to entomology.

- Caroline Lucretia Herschel (1750–1848) was a German-British astronomer and the sister of astronomer Sir William Herschel (1738–1822). They both worked throughout their careers. Caroline's most significant contribution to astronomy was the discovery of several comets and, in particular, the periodic comet 35P/Herschel–Rigollet.

Although the traditional stereotypes against women were still in swing in the nineteenth century, the number of women's recorded contributions to science began to grow. In the latter part of this century, women's educational opportunities began to excel as Western societies began to give priority in establishing schools for girls similar to those of boys. In the UK, for example, many schools were founded, such as the North London Collegiate School (1850), Cheltenham Ladies' College (1853), and the Girls' Public Day School Trust schools (from 1872). The first UK women's university college, Girton, was founded in 1869 and others soon followed: Newnham (1871) and Somerville (1879).

During this period, many co-educational (mixed-sex education) colleges and universities were also founded or started to accept women. In the United States, Catherine Elizabeth Benson, née Brewer (1822–1908), became the first woman to earn a college bachelor's degree. She entered Georgia Female College (now Wesleyan College) in 1839. The college, chartered in 1836, began offering classes in 1839. The honour of being the first woman to earn a degree from a chartered college fell to her because her name came first alphabetically among the graduates of the class of 1840. Elizabeth Bragg became the first woman to graduate with a civil engineering degree in the United States, from the University of California, Berkeley, in 1876.

Recorded examples of women in science in the nineteenth century include

- Mary Fairfax Somerville (1780–1872) was a Scottish science writer and polymath. She studied mathematics and astronomy and was the second woman scientist to receive recognition in the United Kingdom after Caroline Herschel. Mary carried out experiments in magnetism, presenting a paper entitled 'The Magnetic Properties of the Violet Rays of the Solar Spectrum' to the Royal Society in 1826, only the second woman to do so. She also authored several mathematical, astronomical, physical, and geographical texts and was a strong advocate for women's education. In 1835, she and Caroline Herschel were the first two women to be elected to the Royal Astronomical Society.

- Maria Mitchell (1818–1889) was an American astronomer who, in 1847, by using a telescope, discovered a comet which as a result became known as the Miss Mitchell's Comet. She won a gold medal prize for her discovery which was presented to her by King Frederick VII of Denmark. The medal said, 'Not in vain do we watch the setting and rising of the stars'. Mitchell was the first American woman to work as a professional astronomer. She also contributed calculations to the Nautical Almanac produced by the United States Naval Observatory. She became the first woman member of the American Academy of Arts and Sciences in 1848 and of the American Association for the Advancement of Science in 1850.

- Mary Anning (1799–1847) was a British palaeontologist and fossil collector who became known around the world for a number of important finds she made in the Jurassic marine fossil beds in her home county of Dorset, at Lyme Regis. Her work contributed to fundamental changes that occurred during her lifetime in scientific thinking about prehistoric life and the history of the earth.

- Anna Atkins (1799–1871) was an English botanist and photographer. She is considered the first person to publish a book illustrated with photographic images. Other sources claim that she was the first woman to create a photograph.

- Jeanne Villepreux-Power (1794–1871) was a pioneering female French marine biologist. She was the first person to create an aquaria (aquarium) for experimenting with aquatic organisms in 1832.

- Annie Scott Dill Maunder, née Russell (1868–1947), was an Irish astronomer and mathematician. She was a pioneer in astronomical photography, especially of sunspots. She was an assistant to the English astronomer Edward Walter Maunder (1851–1928), who was the head of the solar department at the Royal Greenwich Observatory or RGO and renowned for his study of sunspots and the solar magnetic cycle that led to his identification of the period from 1645 to 1715 that is now known as the Maunder Minimum (also known as the prolonged sunspot minimum).

- Phoebe Sarah Hertha Ayrton, née Marks (1854–23 August 1923) was an English engineer, mathematician, and inventor. In the late nineteenth century, electric arc lighting was in wide use for public lighting. The tendency of electric arcs to flicker and hiss was a major problem. In 1895, Hertha Ayrton wrote a series of articles for *The*

Electrician, explaining that these phenomena were the result of oxygen coming into contact with the carbon rods used to create the arc. In 1899, she was the first woman ever to read her own paper before the Institution of Electrical Engineers (IEE). Shortly thereafter, she was elected the first female member of the IEE.

- Margaret Lindsay, Lady Huggins (1848–1915), was an Irish scientific investigator and amateur astronomer. With her husband William Huggins, she was a pioneer in the field of spectroscopy.

- Dorothea Klumpke Roberts (1861–1942) was an astronomer. Despite being a woman, and in the face of fierce competition from fifty men, she secured the post of director of the Bureau of Measurements at the Paris Observatory. She was the first recipient of the Prix de Dames from the Société des Astronomique de France in 1889 and, in 1893, was made an Officier d'Académe of the French Academy of Sciences—up to that time, these honours had not been awarded to a woman.

- Koncordie Amalie Dietrich (1821–1891) was a German naturalist who was best known for her pioneering work in Australia, where she spent ten years collecting specimens for the Museum Godeffroy in Hamburg.

- Agnes Luise Wilhelmine Pockels (1862–1935) was a German pioneer in chemistry.

Recorded examples of women in science in the twentieth century include

- Alice Perry became the first woman to graduate with a degree in civil engineering in Ireland or Great Britain in 1906 from Queen's College, Galway, Ireland.

- Lise Meitner (1878–1968) was an Austrian, later Swedish, physicist who worked on radioactivity and nuclear physics. She was part of the team that discovered nuclear fission in 1939.

- Inge Lehmann (1888–1993) was a Danish seismologist. In 1936, she argued that the earth's core is not one single molten sphere but that an inner core exists which has physical properties that are different from those of the outer core.

- Ellen Henrietta Swallow Richards (1842–1911) was the foremost female industrial and environmental chemist in the United States in the nineteenth century, pioneering the field of home economics. Richards graduated from Westford Academy (second oldest secondary school in Massachusetts). She was the first woman admitted to the Massachusetts Institute of Technology and its first female instructor, the first woman in America accepted to any school of science and technology, and the first American woman to earn a degree in chemistry.

- Annie Jump Cannon (11 December 1863–13 April 1941) was an American astronomer whose cataloguing work was instrumental in the development of contemporary stellar classification. With Edward C. Pickering, she is credited with the creation of the Harvard Classification Scheme, which was the first serious attempt to organise and classify stars based on their temperatures. In astronomy today, stars are organised and classified in order: O, B, A, F, G, K, M.

- Henrietta Swan Leavitt (4 July 1868–12 December 1921) was an American astronomer. In 1893, she went to work at the Harvard College Observatory in a menial capacity as a 'computer', assigned to count images on photographic plates. Study of the plates led Leavitt to a groundbreaking discovery, worked out while she laboured as a $10.50-a-week assistant, which made possible in turn the pivotal discoveries of astronomer Edwin Hubble. Leavitt's formulation of the period-luminosity relationship of cepheid variable stars provided the foundation for a paradigm shift in modern astronomy, an accomplishment for which she received almost no recognition during her lifetime.

- Cecilia Payne-Gaposchkin (1900–1979) was an English-American astronomer who in 1925 was first to show that the sun is mainly composed of hydrogen, contradicting accepted wisdom at the time.

- Maud Leonora Menten (1879–1960) was a Canadian medical scientist who made significant contributions to enzyme kinetics and immunohistochemistry or IHC. In biochemistry, she is strongly linked with the famous Michaelis-Menten equation.

- The American nutritionists Lydia J. Roberts, Hazel K. Stiebeling, and Helen S. Mitchell developed the recommended dietary allowance in 1941 to help military and civilian groups make plans for group-feeding situations. The RDAs proved necessary, especially, once food began to be rationed.

- Rachel Louise Carson (1907–1964) was an American marine biologist and conservationist. Her book *Silent Spring* (published 1962) and other writings are credited with advancing the global environmental movement.

- Eugenie Clark (born 4 May 1922), sometimes referred to as the Shark Lady, is an American ichthyologist known for her research on poisonous fish of the tropical seas and

- Maria Goeppert-Mayer (1906–1972) was a German-born American theoretical physicist. She is the second female laureate in physics, after Marie Curie. In 1963, she was awarded the Nobel Prize in Physics for developing a mathematical model for the structure of nuclear shells.

The Nobel Prize in Chemistry

- Marie Skłodowska-Curie was the sole winner of the 1911 Nobel Prize in Chemistry. She was the first woman to win a Nobel Prize, the only woman to date to win in two fields, and the only person to win in multiple sciences.

- Irène Joliot-Curie (1897–1956) was a French scientist, the daughter of Marie Skłodowska-Curie and Pierre Curie and the wife of Frédéric Joliot-Curie. Jointly with her husband, Joliot-Curie was awarded the Nobel Prize for chemistry in 1935 for their discovery of artificial radioactivity.

- Dorothy Mary Hodgkin (1910–1994), née Crowfoot, was a British chemist, credited with the development of protein crystallography or X-ray crystallography, a method used to determine the three dimensional structures of biomolecules. Among her most influential discoveries are the confirmation of the structure of penicillin that Ernst Boris Chain had previously surmised and then the structure of vitamin B_{12} for which she was awarded the 1964 Nobel Prize in Chemistry.

- Ada E. Yonath (born 22 June 1939) is an Israeli crystallographer best known for her pioneering work on the structure of the ribosome. She shared the 2009 Nobel Prize in Chemistry with Venkatraman Ramakrishnan and Thomas A. Steitz for her studies on the structure and function of the ribosome. This made her the first woman from the Middle East to win a Nobel Prize in the sciences.

The Nobel Prize in Physiology or Medicine

- Gerty Theresa Cori, née Radnitz (1896–1957), was an American biochemist who became the third woman and the first American woman to award a Nobel Prize in science. She was also and the first woman to be awarded the Nobel Prize in Physiology or Medicine in 1947. She was the recipient of the award together with her husband, Bernardo Houssayf, or the discovery of the mechanism by which glycogen—a derivative of glucose—is broken down in muscle tissue into lactic acid and then resynthesized in the body and stored as a source of energy (known as the Cori cycle).

- Rosalyn Sussman Yalow (1921–2011) was an American medical physicist. She shared her 1977 Nobel Prize in Physiology or Medicine with Roger Guillemin and Andrew Schally for the development of the radioimmunoassay (RIA) technique. She was the second American woman to be awarded the Nobel Prize in Physiology or Medicine after Gerty Cori.

- Barbara McClintock (1902–1992) is an American scientist and one of the world's most distinguished cytogeneticists. In 1983, she was awarded the Nobel Prize in Physiology or Medicine, awarded to her for the discovery of genetic transposition—the only woman to receive an unshared Nobel Prize in that category.

- Rita Levi-Montalcini (born 22 April 1909) is an Italian neurologist who, along with colleague Stanley Cohen, received the 1986 Nobel Prize in Physiology or Medicine for their discovery of nerve growth factor (NGF). Since 2001, she has also served in the Italian Senate as a senator for life.

- Gertrude Belle Elion (1918–1999) was an American biochemist and pharmacologist. In 1988, she was awarded the Nobel Prize in Physiology or Medicine. Elion developed many new drugs, using innovative research methods that would later lead to the development of the AIDS drug AZT.

- Christiane Nüsslein-Volhard (born 20 October 1942) is a German biologist who won the Albert Lasker Award for Basic Medical Research in 1991 and the Nobel Prize in Physiology or Medicine in 1995, along with Eric Wieschaus and Edward B. Lewis, for their research on the genetic control of embryonic development.

- Linda Brown Buck (born 29 January 1947) is an American biologist best known for her work on the olfactory system. She was awarded the 2004 Nobel Prize in Physiology or Medicine, together with Richard Axel, for their work on olfactory receptors.

- Françoise Barré-Sinoussi (born 30 July 1947) is a French virologist and director of the Regulation of Retroviral Infections at the Institut Pasteur in Paris, France. Barré-Sinoussi pioneered some of the fundamental work in the identification of the human immunodeficiency virus (HIV) as the cause of AIDS. In 2008, she was awarded the Nobel Prize in Physiology or Medicine, along with Luc Montagnier, for their discovery of HIV 2004.

- Elizabeth Helen Blackburn (born 26 November 1948) is an Australian-born American biological researcher at the University of California, San Francisco, who studies the telomere, a structure at the end of chromosomes that protects the chromosome. Blackburn co-discovered telomerase, the enzyme that replenishes the telomere. For this work, she shared the 2009 Nobel Prize in Physiology or Medicine with Jack W. Szostak and Carol W. Greider (born 15 April 1961), who is a numbered female winner of the prestigious award. Carol W. Greider is an American molecular biologist. She is a Daniel Nathans Professor and Director of Molecular Biology and Genetics at Johns Hopkins University. She discovered the enzyme telomerase in 1984, when she was a graduate student of Elizabeth Blackburn at the University of California, Berkeley. Greider pioneered research on the structure of telomeres, the ends of the chromosomes.

Chapter 40

Women's Contribution to Mathematics

C oncerning the history of mathematics, providing that women have been traditionally constraint academically, males have long dominated the field. There has been, however, a long history of women in the mathematics, albeit they have been underrepresented as a minority to men who form the majority. But since the late nineteenth century, there is an increase in the initiation of women entering into mathematics. In spite of the gender-based barriers, many women mathematicians have made significant contributions to the field.

Notable female mathematicians include

- Hypatia (c. AD 350–370–March 415) was a Greek Neoplatonist philosopher in Roman Egypt who was the first historically noted woman in mathematics. As head of the Platonist school at Alexandria, she also taught philosophy and astronomy.

- Marie-Sophie Germain (1776–1831) was a French mathematician, physicist, and philosopher. She educated herself from books in her father's library and from correspondence with famous mathematicians such as

LaGrange, Legendre, and Gauss. As one of the pioneers of the elasticity theory, she became the first woman to win a prize from the Paris Academy of Sciences for her essay on the subject in 1816. Germain's work on Fermat's Last Theorem (in number theory, Fermat's Last Theorem states that no three positive integers a, b, and c can satisfy the equation $a^n + b^n = c^n$ for any integer value of n greater than two) provided a foundation for mathematicians exploring the subject for centuries years after.

- Sofia Vasilyevna Kovalevskaya (1850–1891) was the first major Russian female mathematician responsible for important original contributions to analysis, differential equations, and mechanics, and the first woman appointed to a full professorship in Northern Europe. She was also one of the first females to work for a scientific journal as an editor.

- Maria Gaetana Agnesi (1718–1799) was an Italian linguist, mathematician, and philosopher. Agnesi is credited with writing the first book discussing both differential and integral calculus (a branch of mathematics focused on limits, functions, derivatives, integrals, and infinite series). She was an honorary member of the faculty at the University of Bologna.

- Amalie Emmy Noether (1882–1935) was an influential German mathematician known for her groundbreaking contributions to abstract algebra and theoretical physics. She revolutionized the theories of rings, fields, and algebras. Amalie is considered by many as the most important woman in the history of mathematics.

- Grace Alele-Williams (born 16 December 1932) was the first Nigerian woman to become the head (vice chancellor) of a Nigerian university, the University of Benin in 1985. She served as its vice chancellor until 1991.

- Annie Dale Biddle Andrews (1885–1940) was the first woman to earn a PhD in mathematics from the University of California, Berkeley.

- Alexandra Bellow (born 30 August 1935) is a mathematician from Bucharest, Romania, who has made substantial contributions to the fields of ergodic theory, probability, and analysis.

- Vasanti N. Bhat-Nayak (1938–2009) was a professor of combinatorics and head of the department of mathematics, University of Mumbai. Vasanti Nayak was known for her work in BIBD designs, bivariegated graphs, graceful graphs, graph equations, and frequency partitions.

- Dorothy Lewis Bernstein (1914–1988) was an American mathematician known for her work in applied mathematics, statistics, computer programming, and her research on the Laplace transform.

- Gertrude Blanch (*c.*1897–1996) was an American mathematician who did pioneering work in numerical analysis and computation.

- Marjorie Lee Browne (1914–1979) was a notable mathematics educator, the second African American woman to receive a doctoral degree in the US and one of the first black women to receive a doctorate in mathematics in the US.

- Dame Mary Lucy Cartwright (1900–1998) was a leading twentieth century British mathematician.

- Marie Crous (date of birth unknown, date of death unknown) was a French mathematician. She introduced the decimal system to France in the seventeenth century.

- Cypra Cecilia Krieger-Dunaij (1894–1974) was an Austro-Hungarian mathematician. In 1930, Krieger became the third person (and first woman) to earn a PhD in mathematics from a university in Canada, as well as the third woman to have been awarded a doctorate in any discipline in Canada.

- Olga Aleksandrovna Ladyzhenskaya (1922–2004) was a Soviet and Russian mathematician. She was known for her work on partial differential equations and fluid dynamics. She provided the first rigorous proofs of the convergence of a finite difference method for the Navier-Stokes equations.

- Florence Jessie MacWilliams (1917–1990) was an English mathematician who contributed to the field of coding theory.

- Winifred Edgerton (1862–1951) was the first American woman to receive a PhD in mathematics. She was awarded the PhD with high honours from Columbia University in 1886.

- Evelyn Merle Nelson (1943–1987) was a Canadian mathematician. Nelson made contributions to the area of universal algebra with applications to theoretical computer science. Together with Cecilia Krieger, she is the namesake of the Krieger–Nelson Prize, awarded by the Canadian Mathematical Society for outstanding research by a female mathematician since 1995.

- Johanna (Hanna) Neumann (1914–1971) was a German-born mathematician who worked on group theory.

Chapter 41

Women's Contribution to Computing

omputer technology is the most intrinsic part of modern civilisation. Without computers the advanced progress and development of this world would rather be a matter of speculation. Computing is, today, vital to information societies, whereby the creations, distribution, diffusion, use, integration, and manipulation of information is a significant economic, political, and cultural activity. Be it known that the English mathematician Augusta Ada King, Countess of Lovelace (1815–1852), devised a method of using punched cards to calculate Bernoulli numbers which is recognised as the first algorithm intended to be processed by a machine. This is considered the first computer programmer. In 1980, the US Department of Defense named its computer language Ada in her honour. In 1843, she also wrote a scientific paper that anticipated the development of computer software artificial intelligence and computer music.

To this information age, also commonly known as the computer age or digital age, women have made significant contributions. Recorded examples of women's contributions to computing include

- Rear Admiral Grace Murray Hopper (1906–1992), who was one of the first programmers of the Harvard Mark I, the IBM Automatic Sequence Controlled Calculator

(ASCC) computer, and developed the first compiler for a computer programming language.

- Kathleen 'Kay' McNulty Mauchly Antonelli (1921–2006), Marlyn Meltzer, Jean Bartik (1924–2011), Frances Elizabeth 'Betty' Holberton (1917–2001), Frances Spence (b.1922), and Ruth Teitelbaum (1924–1986) were six of the original programmers for the Electronic Numerical Integrator and Computer (ENIAC), the first general purpose electronic computer.

- The American computer scientist Jean E. Sammet (b.1928) developed the FORMAC programming language (acronym of FORmula MAnipulation Compiler) in 1962. She became the first female president of the Association for Computing Machinery in 1974.

- Mary Allen Wilkes (b.1937) was the first person to use a computer in a private home in 1965. She is also the first developer of an operating system (LAP) for the first minicomputer Laboratory INstrument Computer (LINC).

- Sister Mary Kenneth Keller (1914–1985) was the first American woman to earn a PhD in computer science, from the University of Wisconsin–Madison in 1965. Her thesis was titled 'Inductive Inference on Computer Generated Patterns'.

- Sophie Wilson (b.1957) is a British computer scientist. She is known for designing the Acorn Micro-Computer, the first of a long line of computers sold by Acorn Computers Ltd.

- Frances Elizabeth 'Fran' Allen (b.1932) is an American computer scientist and pioneer in the field of optimizing compilers. Her achievements include seminal work in compilers, code optimization, and parallelization. She also had a role in intelligence work on programming languages and security codes for the National Security Agency. In 1989, Allen was the first female IBM Fellow and the first woman to win the Turing Award in 2006.

- Shafrira Goldwasser (b.1958) is a professor of electrical engineering and computer science at MIT and a professor of mathematical sciences at the Weizmann Institute of Science, Israel. She has twice won the Gödel Prize in theoretical computer science: first in 1993 (for 'The knowledge complexity of interactive proof systems') and again in 2001 (for 'Interactive Proofs and the Hardness of Approximating Cliques').

- Anita Borg (1949–2003) was an American computer scientist. She founded the Institute for Women and Technology in 1997 (now the Anita Borg Institute for Women and Technology) and the Grace Hopper Celebration of Women in Computing.

- Marissa Ann Mayer (b.1975) is an American business executive and the president and CEO of Yahoo! Mayer was the first female engineer hired by Google in 1999.

- Jeri Ellsworth is an American entrepreneur and self-taught computer-chip designer. She created the C64 Direct-to-TV ('computer in a joystick') in 2004.

Chapter 42

Women's Suffrage and Political Advancement

On a global scale, the last vestiges of sexism, classism, and racism continue to play havoc in the lives of many people. For generations, these diseases have contaminated human societies. These beset hundreds of millions of people with discriminatory practices every day. The downtrodden masses have had to bear many gross injustices in the vicissitudes of life. In the grimmest days, women were disenfranchised from voting and debarred from standing for parliament universally. The actions of male chauvinists and the policies of patriarchal societies have always been unfair towards women.

The practices of hierarchy and aristocracy have for many centuries depraved the poor and have-nots of their human rights. In the history of Europe, I cited many societies denied people the right to vote on the basis of property requirements or other measures of wealth. This gave rise to universal adult male suffrage movements. This eventually obtained the rights of all male citizens to vote, regardless of property ownership or socio-economic status. France is generally recognised as the first national system to abolish all property requirements for voting. France first used universal male suffrage in 1792. The French revolution (1789–1799) was a catalyst for male suffrage in France. Soon after, the sweeping tides of universal male suffrage reached other European countries. But in typical fashion, the old ideas about patriarchy traditions of male aristocracy and religious authorities continued to deny women the opportunities to enjoy the ideals of equality, citizenship, and inalienable rights as men.

During that period, women faced many social, economic, and political upheavals in Europe and throughout the rest of the world. Be mindful that the unjust laws enacted in Europe were a burden to women almost everywhere, as the globe was predominantly colonies of colonial European states. The British Empire, for example, was the empire on which the sun never sets in the nineteenth and early twentieth centuries. Thus, the British global empire was so extensive that there was always at least one of its territories in daylight. However, women were continuously denied the rights to vote and to own and control their own property throughout the world. This merely assured patriarchal hierarchies from the dawn of Europe's civilization continuously to the nineteenth century. Women were so disadvantaged that they were limited in what they could inherit. In accordance with the law, in the United Kingdom for example, real property was often bequeathed to the brothers of females, who would've been willed the moveable properties such as clothing, jewellery, and household furniture.

Upon marriage, furthermore, not only the legal identity of women ceased to exist but their properties were surrendered to their husbands as well. Married women could not draft wills or dispose of any property without their husbands' consent. For the legal doctrine in the common law of England defined the role of the wife as a 'feme covert', referring to the legal status of a married woman. Thus, in common law, coverture was the protection and control of a woman by her husband that gave rise to various rights and obligations.

Upon marriage, a husband and wife were said to have acquired unity of person that resulted in the husband having various rights over the property of his wife. Wives were deprived of power to enter into contracts or to bring lawsuits as an independent person. This law had served to subordinate the wife to her husband, making him her baron or lord. The coverture was practised under the legal system of the United Kingdom and the United States throughout most of the nineteenth century. It wasn't until 1882 when the Parliament of the United Kingdom passed the Married Women's Property Act, which granted to married women the right to own and control their own property.

Unfortunately, the abolition of these marital restrictions did not abrogate the constraint on women to vote. In like manner, women were still prohibited from voting and running for office in the UK, as it were in other countries. As no one can take more than what they can bear, by the late nineteenth century, suffragists began to organise economic and political reform movement aimed at achieving those rights for women, without any restrictions or qualifications such as property ownership, payment of tax, or marital status. In the United Kingdom, the National Society for Women's Suffrage, formed in 1867 by Lydia Ernestine Becker (1827–1890), was the first national group to campaign for women's right to vote. This organisation helped lay the foundations for women's suffrage movement in Britain and other parts of the world. The campaign for women's suffrage was furthered by the National Union of Women's Suffrage Societies and the Women's Social and Political Union. During this time, the British suffragist Emmeline Pankhurst was one of the leading advocators who travelled constantly, giving speeches throughout Britain and the United States. One of her most famous speeches, 'Freedom or death', was delivered in Connecticut in 1913.

By the early twentieth century, campaigns for women's suffrage were sweeping across the Western World. But with the deadly outbreak of the First World War in 1914, much of the campaigns were halted in most of the West. Prior to this, though, women in Norway received suffrage in 1913. Nonetheless, women's suffrage came before the end of the war in most European nations. In 1915, women in Denmark and in the remaining Australian states won the right to vote. Near the end of the war, Canada, Soviet Russia, Germany, and Poland also recognised women's right to participate in the elective franchise. British women over 30 gained the right to vote in 1918, Dutch women in 1919, and American women won the suffrage in 1920. Women in Turkey won voting rights in 1926. In 1928, British women won suffrage on the same terms as men, that is, for persons 21 years old and older.

Some countries adopted women's suffrage later on in the twentieth century such as France in 1944 and Switzerland in 1971. This is attributable to the United Nations' Human Rights Commission constituting voting rights for women international law. In 1948, the United Nations adopted the Universal Declaration of Human Rights; Article 21 stated: (1) 'Everyone has the right to take part in the government of his country, directly or through freely chosen representatives.' (3) 'The will of the people shall be the basis of the authority of government; this will shall be expressed in periodic and genuine elections which shall be by universal and equal suffrage and shall be held by secret vote or by equivalent free voting procedures.' The United Nations General Assembly adopted the Convention on the Political Rights of Women, which went into force in 1954, ensuring the equal rights of women to vote, hold office, and access public services as set out by national laws.

New Zealand is credited as the first country to grant unrestricted women's suffrage in the general election of 1893. Meanwhile South Africa was one of the last UN nations to grant unrestricted suffrage, with the abrogation of the apartheid system and the first free multiparty elections in 1994. This was won by the African National Congress (ANC) led by Nelson Rolihlahla Mandela, who then became the first ever president to be elected in a fully representative democratic election. As the wife of Nelson, Winnie

Mandela was the first native African woman to be the First Lady of South Africa. Since then, Winnie has held several government positions in South Africa.

Since universal suffrage, women have not only utilized their right to vote but also to hold legislative office on the same basis as men. Women have heretofore and still are fulfilling their political ambitions through the world. Although patriarchy has not disappeared, but merely changed form in many countries, women continue to strive against the odds to be ascended to the highest position of government. Throughout the world, women have been elected and appointed as heads of government of their respective countries. In addition, many women have been elected or appointed as heads of state and deputy heads of state of their respective countries. Many political offices in the United Nations and European Union have been held by women.

To consolidate the political progress of women, Icelandic female politician, Vigdís Finnbogadóttir, established the Council of Women World Leaders in 1996. The council is a network of current and former women prime ministers and presidents. The council's mission is to mobilize the highest-level women leaders globally for collective action on issues of critical importance to women. The council is a policy programme of the Woodrow Wilson International Center for Scholars. Located in Washington, DC, it is a United States presidential memorial that was established as part of the Smithsonian Institution by an act of Congress in 1968. The centre is named in honour of President Woodrow Wilson (the only President of the United States with a PhD).

List of female heads of state

Name	Country	Office	Assumed Office	Mandate end
Sirimavo Bandaranaike	Ceylon	Prime Minister	1960-07-21	1965-03-27
Indira Gandhi	India	Prime Minister	1966-01-24	1977-04-24
Golda Meir	Israel	Prime Minister	1969-03-17	1974-06-03
Sirimavo Bandaranaike	Ceylon	Prime Minister	1970-05-29	1972-05-22
Sirimavo Bandaranaike	Sri Lanka	Prime Minister	1972-05-22	1977-07-23
Isabel Martínez de Perón	Argentina	President	1974-07-01	1976-03-24
Elisabeth Domitien	Central African Republic	Prime Minister	1975-01-02	1976-04-07
Margaret Thatcher	United Kingdom	Prime Minister	1979-05-04	1990-11-28
Maria de Lourdes Pintasilgo	Portugal	Prime Minister	1979-11-01	1980-01-03
Lidia Gueiler Tejada	Bolivia	Acting President	1979-11-16	1980-07-17
Indira Gandhi	India	Prime Minister	1980-01-15	1984-10-31
Eugenia Charles	Dominica	Prime Minister	1980-07-21	1995-06-14
Gro Harlem Brundtland	Norway	Prime Minister	1981-02-04	1981-10-14
Maria Lea Pedini-Angelini	San Marino	Captain Regent	1981-04-01	1981-10-01
Milka Planinc	Yugoslavia	Prime Minister	1982-05-16	1986-5-15
Gloriana Ranocchini	San Marino	Captain Regent	1984-04-01	1984-10-01
Corazon Aquino	Philippines	President	1986-02-25	1992-06-30
Gro Harlem Brundtland	Norway	Prime Minister	1986-05-09	1989-10-16
Benazir Bhutto	Pakistan	Prime Minister	1988-12-02	1990-7-6
Gloriana Ranocchini	San Marino	Captain Regent	1989-10-1	1990-4-1
Ertha Pascal-Trouillot	Haiti	Acting President	1990-03-13	1991-02-07
Kazimira Prunskienė	Lithuania	Prime Minister	1990-03-11	1991-01-10
Violeta Chamorro	Nicaragua	President	1990-04-25	1997-01-10
Gro Harlem Brundtland	Norway	Prime Minister	1990-11-03	1996-10-25

Khaleda Zia	Bangladesh	Prime Minister	1991-03-20	1996-3-30
Édith Cresson	France	Prime Minister	1991-05-15	1992-04-02
Edda Ceccoli	San Marino	Captain Regent	1991-10-01	1992-04-01
Hanna Suchocka	Poland	Prime Minister	1992-7-11	1993-10-25
Patricia Busignani	San Marino	Captain Regent	1993-04-01	1993-10-01
Tansu Çiller	Turkey	Prime Minister	1993-06-13	1996-03-06
Kim Campbell	Canada	Prime Minister	1993-6-25	1993-11-4
Sylvie Kinigi	Burundi	Prime Minister	1993-07-10	1993-10-27
Agathe Uwilingiyimana	Rwanda	Prime Minister	1993-07-18	1994-04-07
Benazir Bhutto	Pakistan	Prime Minister	1993-10-19	1996-11-05
Sylvie Kinigi	Burundi	Acting President	1993-10-27	1994-02-07
Reneta Indzhova	Bulgaria	Acting Prime Minister	1994-10-17	1995-01-25
Chandrika Kumaratunga	Sri Lanka	Prime Minister	1994-08-19	1994-11-14
Sirimavo Bandaranaike	Sri Lanka	Prime Minister	1994-11-14	2000-07-10
Claudette Werleigh	Haiti	Prime Minister	1995-11-07	1996-02-27
Hasina Wazed	Bangladesh	Prime Minister	1996-06-23	2001-07-15
Ruth Perry	Liberia	Chairperson of the Council of State	1996-09-03	1997-08-02
Rosalía Arteaga Serrano	Ecuador	Acting President	1997-02-09	1997-02-11
Janet Jagan	Guyana	Prime Minister	1997-03-06	1997-12-19
Jenny Shipley	New Zealand	Prime Minister	1997-12-05	1999-12-05
Anne Enger	Norway	Acting Prime Minister	1998-08-30	1998-09-23
Rosa Zafferani	San Marino	Captain Regent	1999-04-01	1999-10-01
Irena Degutienė	Lithuania	Acting Prime Minister	1999-05-04	1999-05-18
Nyam-Osoryn Tuyaa	Mongolia	Acting Prime Minister	1999-07-22	1999-07-30
Mireya Moscoso	Panama	President	1999-09-10	2004-09-01
Irena Degutienė	Lithuania	Acting Prime Minister	1999-10-27	1999-11-03
Helen Clark	New Zealand	Prime Minister	1999-12-05	2008-11-19
Maria Domenica Michelotti	San Marino	Captain Regent	2000-04-01	2000-10-01

Gloria Macapagal-Arroyo	Philippines	President	2001-01-20	2010-06-30
Mame Madior Boye	Senegal	Prime Minister	2001-03-03	2002-11-04
Megawati Sukarnoputri	Indonesia	President	2001-07-23	2004-10-20
Khaleda Zia	Bangladesh	Prime Minister	2001-10-10	2006-10-29
Chang Sang	South Korea	Acting Prime Minister	2002-07-11	2002-07-31
Maria das Neves	São Tomé and Príncipe	Prime Minister	2002-10-03	2004-09-18
Anneli Jäätteenmäki	Finland	Prime Minister	2003-04-17	2003-06-24
Beatriz Merino	Peru	Prime Minister	2003-06-28	2003-12-15
Valeria Ciavatta	San Marino	Captain Regent	2003-10-01	2004-4-1
Luisa Diogo	Mozambique	Prime Minister	2004-02-17	2010-01-16
Radmila Šekerinska	Macedonia	Acting Prime Minister	2004-05-12	2004-06-12
Radmila Šekerinska	Macedonia	Acting Prime Minister	2004-11-03	2004-12-15
Yulia Tymoshenko	Ukraine	Prime Minister	2005-01-24	2005-009-6
Fausta Morganti	San Marino	Captain Regent	2005-04-01	2005-10-01
Cynthia Pratt	Bahamas	Acting Prime Minister	2005-05-04	2005-06-06
Maria do Carmo Silveira	São Tomé and Príncipe	Prime Minister	2005-06-08	2006-04-21
Angela Merkel	Germany	Chancellor	2005-11-22	Incumbent
Ellen Johnson Sirleaf	Liberia	President	2006-01-16	Incumbent
Michelle Bachelet	Chile	President	2006-03-11	2010-03-11
Portia Simpson-Miller	Jamaica	Prime Minister	2006-03-30	2007-09-11
Han Myeong-sook	South Korea	Prime Minister	2006-04-19	2007-03-07
Cristina Fernández de Kirchner	Argentina	President	2007-12-10	Incumbent
Yulia Tymoshenko	Ukraine	Prime Minister	2007-12-18	2010-03-03
Zinaida Greceanîi	Moldova	Prime Minister	2008-03-31	2009-09-14
Rosa Zafferani	San Marino	Captain Regent	2008-04-01	2008-10-01
Michèle Pierre-Louis	Haiti	Prime Minister	2008-09-05	2009-11-11
Assunta Meloni	San Marino	Captain Regent	2008-10-01	2009-4-1
Hasina Wazed	Bangladesh	Prime Minister	2009-01-06	Incumbent

Jóhanna Sigurðardóttir	Iceland	Prime Minister	2009-02-01	Incumbent
Jadranka Kosor	Croatia	Prime Minister	2009-07-06	2011-12-23
Cécile Manorohanta	Madagascar	Acting Prime Minister	2009-12-18	2009-12-20
Roza Otunbayeva	Kyrgyzstan	President	2010-04-07	2010-12-17
Laura Chinchilla	Costa Rica	President	2010-05-08	2014-05-08
Kamla Persad-Bissessar	Trinidad and Tobago	Prime Minister	2010-05-26	Incumbent
Mari Kiviniemi	Finland	Prime Minister	2010-06-22	2011-06-22
Julia Gillard	Australia	Prime Minister	2010-06-24	2013-06-27
Iveta Radičová	Slovakia	Prime Minister	2010-07-08	2012-04-04
Dilma Rousseff	Brazil	President	2010-10-31	Incumbent
Rosario Fernández	Peru	Prime Minister	2011-03-19	2011-07-28
Maria Luisa Berti	San Marino	Captain Regent	2011-04-01	2011-10-01
Cissé Mariam Kaïdama Sidibé	Mali	Prime Minister	2011-04-03	2012-03-22
Yingluck Shinawatra	Thailand	Prime Minister	2011-08-05	2014-05-07
Helle Thorning-Schmidt	Denmark	Prime Minister	2011-10-03	Incumbent
Portia Simpson-Miller	Jamaica	Prime Minister	2012-01-05	Incumbent
Adiato Djaló Nandigna	Guinea-Bissau	Acting Prime Minister	2012-02-10	2012-04-12
Joyce Banda	Malawi	President	2012-04-07	2014-05-31
Alenka Bratušek	Slovenia	Prime Minister	2013-03-20	2014-09-18
Sibel Siber	Northern Cyprus	Prime Minister	2013-06-20	2013-09-02
Tatiana Turanskaya	Transnistria	Prime Minister	2013-06-20	Incumbent
Aminata Touré	Senegal	Prime Minister	2013-09-01	2014-07-08
Erna Solberg	Norway	Prime Minister	2013-10-16	Incumbent
Laimdota Straujuma	Latvia	Prime Minister	2014-01-22	Incumbent
Ana Jara	Peru	Prime Minister	2014-07-22	Incumbent

Source: http://en.'wikipedia.org/wiki/
List_of_elected_and_appointed_female_heads_of_state

List of the first female holders of political offices

League of Nations

- Substitute delegate and ambassador to the League of Nations Elena Văcărescu (Romanian French aristocrat writer), 1922

- Permanent delegate and ambassador to the League of Nations Elena Văcărescu, 1924

United Nations

- Head of the section of Welfare Policy Alva Myrdal (Swedish sociologist and politician), 1949

- Chairman of UNESCO's social science section Alva Myrdal, 1950

- President of the United Nations General Assembly Vijaya Lakshmi Pandit (Indian diplomat and politician), 1953

- Permanent representative Agda Rössel (permanent representative of Sweden to the United Nations), 1958

- Head of the United Nations Children's Fund Carol Bellamy (American politician), 1995

- United Nations High Commissioner for Human Rights Mary Robinson (Irish politician), 1997

- Deputy Secretary-General Louise Fréchette (Canadian diplomat and public servant), 1998

- Executive director of the United Nations Human Settlements Programme Anna Tibaijuka (Tanzanian), 2000

- Undersecretary-General Inga-Britt Ahlenius (Swedish auditor and public servant), 2005

- President of the International Court of Justice Rosalyn Higgins (English judge), 2006

- Managing director of the International Monetary Fund Christine Lagarde (French lawyer and politician), 2011

European Union

- President of the European Parliament Simone Veil (French lawyer and politician), 1979

- President-in-Office of the European Council Margaret Thatcher (British politician), 1981

- European Commissioner Christiane Scrivener (French politician) / Vasso Papandreou (Greek politician), 1989

- Leader of the Socialist Group and of any major party Pauline Green (British politician), 1994

- Co-vice president of the European Commission Loyola de Palacio (Spanish politician), 1999

- First vice president of the European Commission Margot Wallström (Swedish social democratic politician and diplomat), 2004

- High representative of the Union for Foreign Affairs and Security Policy Catherine Ashton (British Labour politician), 2009

Chapter 43

Women's Contribution to the Abolition of Slavery and Desegregation

From the early fifteenth century and continuing to the seventeenth century, European explorers and colonisers explored the world, annexing lands. This period became known as the age of discovery, (also known as the age of exploration). It came as a terrible price to the natives of Africa, the Americas, Asia, and Oceania. The age of discovery brought in its wake European colonization of those continents. Africans were consigned to chattel slavery. From the beginning of the age of exploration to the early nineteenth century, west and central Africa in particular were the places to purchase humans as chattels. For over 400 years, kidnapped Africans were shipped in the most inhumane manner to European colonies in the Americas, where they became slaves for colonial economies. An estimated twelve million innocent Africans were shipped to the Americas through the transatlantic slave trade. An estimated four million Africans died in slavery and another two million were estimated to die in the Middle Passage.

On the continent and those scattered by the slave trade in the diaspora, women have played significant roles in the African struggle for emancipation. The slave narrative autobiography of Mary Prince (*c*.1788–after 1833), *The History of Mary Prince* (1831), was the first to be published in the United Kingdom by a black woman. Her account of the firsthand experiences in Devonshire Parish, Bermuda, of the inhumanity of enslavement was fundamental in the Anti-Slavery Society campaign to achieve the Slavery Abolition Act 1833.

Women's participation in the struggle was critical to bring the race to the shores of freedom from the subhuman bondage of enslavement. Women's leadership in resistance movements and revolts was equally fundamental. In Portland Parish, Jamaica, for example, Queen Nanny (c.1686–unknown), was a warrioress of great valour. She led the Windward Maroons against the British colonial forces in the eighteenth century. Nanny was a key player in the 1731 First Maroon War between the Jamaican Maroons and the British. Under Nanny's leadership, allied with her five brothers, the Windward and Leeward Maroons were so unconquerable and undefeatable that the British governor in Jamaica was actually subjugated to sign a peace treaty with the freedom fighters in 1739.

Nanny is one of the earliest leaders of slave resistance in the Americas and one of very few women to have done so. In recognition of her role in the Maroon resistance against the British, the government of Jamaica declared Queen Nanny a national heroine in 1976. She is the only female to be crowned with this honour to date. Her portrait graces the $500 Jamaican dollar bill.

As with the Jamaican Maroons, African spirituality played a key role in most slave resistances. The practice is synonymous with other female leaders such as Cécile Fatiman, who was the mambo (a voodoo priestess) in the voodoo ceremony at Bois Caïman in August 1791, together with Dutty Boukman (or Boukman Dutty) in the role of *houngan* (priest). This ceremony is considered to be the trigger for the Haitian Revolution (1791–1804), which led to the abolition of slavery and independence there, as with Queen

Muhumusa—leader of the Nyabinghi resistance in Rwanda and Uganda against the German and later the British colonialists (between 1850 and 1950).

Queen Nzinga a Mbande was also another courageous leader of the Ndongo and Matamba Kingdoms of the Mbundu people against the Portuguese colonisers in seventeenth century Angola, as with Empress Taytu Betul of Ethiopia against the Italian colonialists in the Battle of Adwa, fought on 1 March 1896.

United States of America

In nineteenth century United States of America, Harriet Tubman (*c.*1820–1913) was a key player in guiding slaves to freedom via a network of secret routes and safe houses known as the Underground Railroad to Free States and Canada. Born Araminta Harriet Ross in slavery in Maryland, Tubman escaped to Philadelphia in 1849, returning to Maryland soon after to rescue her family. Using the Underground Railroad, Tubman made more than thirteen missions to rescue more than seventy slaves. But when the United States Congress enacted the Fugitive Slave Act of 1850, declaring that law officials in Free States to help to recapture all runaway slaves and return them to their masters, Tubman helped leading fugitives farther north into Canada, where slavery was abolished. Travelling by night, Harriet Tubman was an efficient navigator in guiding the slaves to freedom that she was called Moses.

During the time of slavery, women were subjected to rape by their masters and overseers. Also, young females were forced to bear children for generally older slaves with large or muscular physique to produce the best babies for slavery. Yet again, many of their children were separated from them at a young age by their masters who sold their young ones into slavery elsewhere. There is no better testimony to this fact than of Isabella Baumfree (known also by her self-given name Sojourner Truth from 1843 onward). Truth was born (*c*.1797) into slavery in Swartekill, New York, as one of the ten or twelve children born to James and Elizabeth Baumfree. But when she was about 9 years old, Truth, known as Belle, was sold at an auction with a flock of sheep for $100 to the cruel and harsh slaver John Neely. In 1808, Neely sold her for $105, to Martinus Schryver, who sold her in 1810 for $175 to John Dumont.

Around 1815, moreover, Truth met and fell in love with Robert who was a slave from a neighbouring plantation. But back then, slaves could not just get involved in a relationship with each other without their master's consent. Masters were even more hard line on their male slaves engaging in relationship with slave women they did not own because they would not own the children. In consequence, Robert's owner, Catlin, did not only forbid his relationship with Truth but he was also savagely beaten in the backlash. Thereafter, Truth never saw Robert again. Truth was later forced by Dumont to marry an older slave named Thomas with whom she had five children.

Truth escaped slavery with her infant daughter Sophia around 1826. After gaining her freedom in 1827, Truth went to court to recover her son that was sold away into slavery, becoming the first woman of African descent to win such a case against a white man. Sojourner Truth became an abolitionist and women's rights activist. She was a well-known anti-slavery orator. But she is best known for her speech on gender inequalities, 'Ain't I a Woman?', which was delivered in 1851 at the Ohio Women's Rights Convention in Akron, Ohio.

European Female Abolitionist

During the inhuman days of slavery, very few of the European Christian people saw the practice as the evil which it represents. The abolition of slavery has been largely due to the decisive and resolute actions of white anti-slavery activists in the Anti-Slavery Society of Great Britain and the United States. These organisations were committed to the abolition of slavery, in particular the British Empire. The Quakers were the first whites to denounced slavery in the American colonies and Europe. From early 1688, the Quakers played a pivotal role in the abolition movement against slavery. The Quakers were also prominently involved with the Underground Railroad as well as the American Anti-Slavery Society (1833–1870) and the Society for the Relief of Free Negroes Unlawfully Held in Bondage (commonly referred to as the Pennsylvania Abolition Society), which was initially formed in 1775.

Because of the systematic subordination of women, the early American and British abolitionists were mostly males. It wasn't until the nineteenth century before women became prominent figures in the anti-slavery movements. Some women in America became well known for their involvement in the abolition of slavery. These women combined suffrage and feminism with the anti-slavery campaign. Lucy Stone (1818–1893), for example, was a prominent American abolitionist and suffragist. Stone was the first woman from Massachusetts to obtain a college degree in 1847. She was the first recorded American woman to retain her own last name after marriage. At a time when women were barred from raising their voice of dissent in public, Stone was a very vocal advocator for women's rights and against slavery.

There were also other prominent female American abolitionists and suffragists, including Paulina Kellogg Wright Davis (1813–1876), Abby Kelley Foster (1811–1887), Maria W. Stewart (Maria Miller) (1803–1880), Sarah Mapps Douglass (1806–1882), Charlotte Forten Grimké (1837–1914), Margaretta Forten (1806–1875), Sarah Parker Remond (1826–1894), Susan Brownell Anthony (1820–1906), Lucretia Coffin Mott (1793–1880), Maria White Lowell (1821–1853), and others. Many of these ladies are affiliated with the American Anti-Slavery Society and the Boston Female Anti-Slavery Society (1833–1840). Leaders of BFASS included Lucy M. Ball, Martha Violet Ball, Mary G. Chapman, Eunice Davis, Mary S. Parker, Sophia Robinson, Henrietta Sargent, T. Southwick,

Catherine M. Sullivan, Anne Warren Weston, Caroline Weston, and Maria Weston Chapman.

In Britain, Hannah More (1745–1833) was a prominent campaigner against the slave trade. In actuality, More together with other male anti-slave-trade activists such as Thomas Clarkson, Granville Sharp, and Charles Middleton were the ones who persuaded William Wilberforce to lead the parliamentary cause of abolition. These individuals and others were the leading British abolitionists behind the Slave Trade Act 1807, passed by the parliament of the United Kingdom on 25 March 1807. This Act only made illegal the trafficking of slaves in the British Empire. But slavery itself, remained legal in the British Empire until the Slavery Abolition Act 1833 and 1838.

For the emancipation of enslaved Africans in the British West Indies, Elizabeth Heyrick (1769–1831) was a strong advocator. As an anti-slavery campaigner, she published a pamphlet entitled 'Immediate, not Gradual Abolition' in 1824. Many other women have played significant roles in the early nineteenth century anti-slavery movement in Britain. But typically, their names have not been listed in the history book of the campaign.

Strong Women in Desegregation

Unfortunately, after the abolition of slavery, many other oppressive treatments were initiated by the colonial policymakers in most of the former slave colonies. In consequence, people of African descent faced all manner of discrimination on the basis of their social class. In the United States of America, for instance, the Thirteenth Amendment, which took effect in December 1865, abolished slavery and involuntary servitude, except as punishment for a crime. Thereafter, each state of the former confederacy codified laws known as the Black Codes, which limited the basic human rights and civil liberties of former slaves. These codes were rooted in the slave codes.

The Black Codes later gave way to the enactment of Jim Crow laws between 1876 and 1965. The Jim-Crowed southern states mandated de jure racial segregation of all public schools, public places, and public transportation, housing, and the segregation of restrooms, restaurants, and drinking fountains for whites and blacks. Jim Crowism constituted superiority for white Americans, while systematizing inferiority for Afro-Americans at a level of society. However, women of African descent in America, as elsewhere, suffered triple oppression—classism, racism, and sexism. Black socialists in the United States developed the triple oppression theory.

The Trinidadian journalist Claudia Cumberbatch Jones (1915–1964) is associated with pioneering the theory. Jones was a political activist and black nationalist through communism from the 1930s until her arrest in 1948, which resulted in her deportation from the US on 7 December 1955. But because of her political and nationalistic affiliations, the then British colonial governor of Trinidad and Tobago denied her entry to the land of her birth. She was eventually offered residency in the United Kingdom on humanitarian grounds. In America, Jones is best remembered for her writing; 'An End to the Neglect of the Problems of the Negro Woman!' appeared in 1949 in *Political Affairs Magazine*. In the UK, Jones is widely regarded as the Mother of the Notting Hill Carnival. She first organised the carnival in January 1959 in St Pancras Town Hall as a response to the 1958 Notting Hill race riots.

During the heyday of overt racially motivated injustices and mistreatments aimed at people of African descent, a lot of protests took place against the vile practices. Throughout the 1930s and 1940s, numerous demonstrations took place against Jim Crow segregations. Rosa Louise McCauley Parks (1913–2005), charged with a so-called act of civil disobedience by refusing to give up her seat on a bus to a white man, triggered the African American Civil Rights Movement (1955–1968). This crime sparked the segregated Afro-Americans into actions that eventually led to the achievement of desegregation and voting rights for them. The civil rights campaign began on 1 December 1955, with the Montgomery Bus Boycott, led by Martin Luther King Jr and Ralph Abernathy, against the policy of racial segregation on the public transit system of Montgomery, Alabama, which constituted Rosa Parks arrest for refusing to surrender her seat to a white person.

The first triumph of the civil rights movement came on 20 December 1956, when a federal ruling, *Browder* v. *Gayle*, took effect and led to a United States Supreme Court decision that declared the Alabama and Montgomery laws requiring segregated buses to be unconstitutional. From there, civil rights activists endured a long and persevering campaign through the rough roads that were paved with the vileness of white supremacy groups, injustices of segregationists, and police brutalities to induce Congress to pass the Civil Rights Act of 1964 and the Voting Rights Act of 1965.

It is truism that beside (more fitting than behind in terms of equality) every successful man there is often a strong woman. In validating the fact, Martin Luther King Jr might've failed to champion the triumph of the African American Civil Rights Movement if his marriage to Coretta Scott King (1927–2006) was unsuccessful. It is equally true that Coretta's undaunted courage had fuelled the flames of Martin's unswerving devotion to the cause of the movement. By his own words, Martin sang the praises of his precious wife, Coretta. Paying tribute to her intestinal fortitude, constant support, and understanding, Martin said: 'My devoted wife has been a constant source of consolation to me through all the difficulties.

'In the midst of the most tragic experiences, she never became panicky or overemotional. I have come to see the real meaning of that rather trite statement: a wife can either make or break a husband. My wife was always stronger than I was through the struggle. While she had certain natural fears and anxieties concerning my welfare, she never allowed them to hamper my active participation in the movement. Corrie proved to be that type of wife with qualities to make a husband when he could have been so easily broken. In the darkest moments, she always brought the light of hope. I am convinced that if I had not had a wife with the fortitude, strength, and calmness of Corrie, I could not have withstood the ordeals and tensions surrounding the movement.

'She saw the greatness of the movement and had a unique willingness to sacrifice herself for its continuation. If I have done anything in this struggle, it is because I have had behind me and at my side a devoted, understanding, dedicated, patient companion in the person of my wife. I can remember times when I sent her away for safety. I would look up a few days later, and she was back home, because she wanted to be there.'[42]

After Martin Luther King Jr was assassinated at the Lorraine Motel in Memphis, Tennessee, on 4 April 1968, Coretta took on prominent role in the leadership of the struggle for desegregation and racial equality. Mrs King was also actively involved in the second-wave feminism in the United States, where it was initially called the Women's Liberation Movement.

In apartheid South Africa, Winnie Mandela was another strong woman that stood by her husband Nelson Mandela, who was a militant anti-apartheid activist. Winnie was a stalwart supporter of the anti-apartheid movement. After Nelson was arrested and sentenced in 1962 to life imprisonment (Mandela went on to serve twenty-serve years in prison, spending many of these years on Robben Island), Winnie with her courage undaunted became a key player in the uproot of the racist and segregated polices of apartheid in South Africa. After inheriting the mantle of leading the disadvantaged South African natives against the white minority

---

[42]   *The Autobiography of Martin Luther King Jr*, 37

rule government, during the early years of her husband's long imprisonment, Winnie was subjected to torturous treatments by the vile apartheid regime. For many of those years, she was exiled to the town of Brandfort in the Orange Free State, with the exception to visit her husband in prison. She also spent eighteen months in solitary confinement at Pretoria Central Prison, which began in 1969. But Winnie Mandela, through her courage and perseverance, managed to overcome all those trials and tribulations to become one of the champion figures of the abrogation of the evil apartheid system.

There were, in addition, many other prominent women in the liberation and reformation movements for people of African descent worldwide. Among these are both wives of Marcus Mosiah Garvey, first wife Ashwood Garvey (1897–1969) and his second wife Amy Euphemia Jacques Garvey (1895–1973). They were strong women beside Garvey in his Pan-African movement.

Many nationalists, Pan-African activists, anti-colonialists, anti-slavery and civil right activists had espoused these movements at grave risk to themselves and their families. In consequence, many have lost their lives and liberty. Many have failed, while others do not live to see that they have succeeded. It is a shame that many of those heroes and heroines are forgotten or unknown by the generations that enjoy the fruits of their labours. It is an act of betrayal to forget those who have sacrificed their all for equity and social justice. Far too often the stories of great men are repeated, whereas the stories of great women who have given their all to make a difference in the lives and prospect of humans are forgotten or remain untold. So let us honour those women who have struggled for the liberty of Africans and people of other races.

Chapter 44

Elevation of Women

The nineteenth and twentieth centuries were great periods for feminism. During those glorious years, feminists raised a storm of women's rights movements. The women's rights subsequently brought the majority of women's issues under the spotlight of world opinion. This storm left a great amount of social, political, academic, and economic reformations in its wake. This era pioneered the elevation of women's access to education, legal rights to own property, and adult suffrage universally. An unprecedented rate of women who had suffered the indignation of gender discrimination was elevated by the waves of feminism. In most countries before these movements, the law did not acknowledge women's rightful status by denying them equal rights as men. These centuries validate the fact that we are able, if willing, to spare women from suffering further humiliation and injustice at the last bastions of gender discrimination.

The concepts of modernity have incited many countries to adopt the policies of democracy, equality, and individual rights. These concepts provide the medium to help humans create peace, understanding, and cooperation in the world. It also provides the medium to help people take into consideration the welfare and well-being of each other. But even in this day and age, women still confront prejudice in the political, economic, and social systems in the Americas, Europe, Africa, Asia, and Oceania.

Because of the long-standing subjection of women in society, unfortunately, it is not yet possible to cite in history an era where the feminine gender is completely free from discriminatory mistreatments. The present burdensome situations of women are the result of traditional sexist ideologies inculcated in the minds of many modern men. The prevailing truth is that, far too many men have yet to be led by rectitude to face the introspection of discriminatory practices. As a result, human societies have yet to facilitate completely the replacement of the dastardly acts of bigotry, maliciousness, intolerance, sexism, and inhuman self-interest with understanding, tolerance, feminism, egalitarianism, and goodwill.

Women today, as in the past, desire to be elevated to the true state of equality at all levels of society. But there are many spurious claims that militate against gender equality. This is because of traditional and individual mal-beliefs which conflict with human rights legislations, denying women the rights that they are inherently and legally entitled. These violations of women's rights are practised in those societies where the governments fail to interfere with the prevailing situations in law. Male chauvinistic pigs often take full advantage of this lawful negligence.

It is a shame that females are still at a disadvantage throughout their lives. From birth, the average girl still faces more hindrance than boys in many modern societies. It is evident that girls are not only raised in a different manner but treated differently than boys. For instance, boys generally gain more playtime than girls. In the societies which harbour the thought of creating good wives, girls are given the bulk of the chores to develop the necessary skills that are viewed suitable to get and keep a 'good husband', who may well treat her no less than a domestic slave. As a direct result, girls, from an early age, are burdened with strenuous work to meet a lifelong of subordinated responsibilities that await them as wives in domesticity.

In connection with these issues are the origins of the attempt of men to assure their dominance of women from the start. Although the ground rules of the traditions of each nation varies, the unprincipled factors which give impetus to the disempowerment of women have been sewed deeply in the fabric of each. The present levels of women's issues are correlated with traditional customs and religious beliefs of men; namely sexism, male chauvinism, and patriarchy. Meanwhile the present status of equality and high standards of living enjoyed by women has been achieved through the relentless endeavours of suffragists and feminists. History amply reveals that organised effort to give women the same economic, social, and political rights as men is not something that can be accomplished neither at one stage nor by coincidence. This level of achievement can neither be reached by one generation but by the result of the toil and sacrifices of succeeding generations. Therefore, if the present generation follow the part of its feminist predecessors, with greater and unceasing zeal, they will not only elevate the position of women in their society but also those inhabiting other parts of the world.

In my study of various social systems of humanity, I have found the treatment of women to be subhuman in many. The reason for the continuity of man's inhumanity to woman lies in the fact that there still remain much to be done to uplift women and girls from the discriminatory rubbles of society. The only way to the elevation of women's social, political, and economic position is through gender parity and empowerment. It is one of the great imperatives of our day for humans to understand that we must eradicate present difficulties to bequeath a better and more just world to the coming generations. We should, therefore, struggle and make sacrifices to ameliorate the wretched conditions of humanity.

Chapter 45

Woman's Rightful Position

D ue to men's reprobate and corrupted minds, they have enmeshed women in a tangle of subordinated bondage in their power struggle. In the light of history, it is blatant that men in their ignorance and sexist ways have failed to grapple with the power of gender parity to humanity. No one can deny that the ultimate strength and progress of humanity can only be at its best result in a synergy of all members of the human family. Because the latent good of which this strength represents is not exploited to the maximum extent for the common good and benefit of humans, the well-being and prosperity of women have been languishing in subordination and lacking in achievements. For no people can be truly happy or make their full contribution to humanity unless they enjoy the fundamental rights and privileges that are prerequisites to obtain the indispensable academic knowledge to render their participation in the significant roles of their societies.

The last forty years have been virtually good for women, though. In this twenty-first century, however, the entire yearnings and hopes of women have yet to be fully realised. Our task, now then, is to prove ourselves worthy of the modern knowledge which we have claimed as our own, capable of rendering solutions to the problems of the universe, which humans have created piecemeal.

The scourges of women are no exception. To this end, we must follow the doctrine of womanitarianism and feminism to advocate for the complete human rights of women and girls.

Deprivation and violation of the international bill of rights for women have resulted in millions of females occupying a marginalised position in many areas of society the world over. We must stand forthright in our support of equal rights for women. We must by steadfast in the urgent imperative of universal abrogation of all repressive customs, gender-based inequalities, violence, and prejudicial actions against women and girls. Such abhorrent acts are too amoral and antiquated for our modern world. Devaluation based on a person's sex is not the way to amity and equality among civilised human beings. Such path lies in the full implementation of the international human rights instruments such as UDHR, ICCPR, ICESCR, CRC, and CEDAW.

Only reprobate individuals endorse the mal-belief that one sex is naturally superior to the other. And thereby should dominate all perceived important aspects of society. This unprincipled ideology has a long-standing history of denying opportunities and human rights to women. Meanwhile the fundamental principle which feminism brings forth is the idea of rights for women equal to those of men. The individuals that are guided by this moral principle can be considered solely essential to human quest for the completion of the foundation laid down for gender equality.

Sexist ideologies are harmful than useful to our societies. For it underlies mistreatment of women and girls. Any doctrine that belittles and holds a group of people in contempt while exalting another, undoubtedly, is an incitement to violence and prejudicial actions. This is meaningless to the good of any society. Equality offers the most solid basis for justice, peace, and harmony among civilised human beings. Sameness of treatment serves society with tolerance and goodwill between all members of the human family. This is useful for peaceful co-existence and the satisfaction of the general interest of society. As a proof, anywhere feminism is not fully applied, women are open to ridicule and mistreatment as the interests of men are not completely coincided with those of women. Apart from this, women's human rights are open to violations. Gender inequality only makes possible for men to apply their discriminatory ideas against women. So without gender equality, the life of hundreds of millions of women and girls will remain hopelessly stagnant. And that is precisely why we should continue to advocate for gender equality. This befits the modern world, with woman in her rightful position of being equal to man.

Chapter 46

Unobtainable Yesterday, Essential Today

Since the waves of feminist movements, it is self-evident that the prospects of women have gradually improved. In many societies today, women and girls have access to opportunities that were previously restricted to their foremothers. Girls have gained more educational opportunities while greater numbers of women are entering the workforce. Women's political prospect has also increased in many countries. As one example, Jamaica elected the nation's first woman head of government in 2006. This came approximately a decade after Violet Nielson became Jamaica's first female speaker in the House of Representatives (1997–2003).

As a Jamaican, I feel proud to observe the role of my foremothers as pioneers especially in the fields of policing and motorcycle. Ionie Ramsay-Nelson became the first female police motorcyclist in 1977. She is also the first Jamaican woman to have risen above the rank of corporal in the traffic division and the first woman to head the traffic section of the Jamaica Constabulary Force in the corporate area. In England, the Jamaican born Sislin Fay Allen was the first woman of African descent to work for the Metropolitan police in 1968. Born in Jamaica, Bessie Stringfield (1911–1993), aka the Motorcycle Queen of Miami, was the first African American woman to ride across the United States alone. She also served as one of the few motorcycle dispatch riders (a military messenger) for the United States military during World War II (1939–1945).

It is for me today a source of immense joy to see women doing what their foremothers were not allowed to do. The entire legal rights of women and girls are enshrined in CEDAW, the international bill of rights for women. Since 1981, CEDAW have defined what constitutes discrimination against women and girls. It also provides the framework for tackling gender inequality. Women's enjoyment of human rights and fundamental freedoms in the political, economic, social, cultural, and civil areas of society were simply unattainable and unheard of less than forty years ago. This meant that if you backdate only to two generations, your mother and grandmothers had experienced firsthand the grim days of gender discrimination and disempowerment.

> Despite ingrained gender inequality, the status of women has improved in the past three decades. An increased awareness of discriminatory practices and outcomes—including physical and sexual violence, female genital mutilation/cutting (FGM/C), disproportionate numbers affected by HIV/AIDS and female illiteracy, among others—has fostered greater demand for change. By promoting legal and social reforms, proponents of gender equality have begun to reshape the social and political landscape. And while gender continues to influence people's choices and challenges, in many parts of the world a girl born in 2007 will probably have a brighter future than a girl born when CEDAW was adopted in 1979.

> Today, women and girls have access to opportunities that were previously restricted. Primary school enrolment rates for girls have jumped and the educational gender gap is

narrowing. Women are entering the labour force in greater numbers. And women's political representation is increasing in many parts of the world.

In 2006, for instance, Chile and Jamaica elected women for the first time as their heads of government. (Chile's president, Michelle Bachelet, is also head of state.) In addition, the Republic of Korea appointed its first woman prime minister in April 2006 . . . While that number is miniscule, considering that there are 192 UN Member States, female government leadership was unheard of less than 50 years ago.

Gains in gender equality not withstanding, far too many women and girls have been left behind and remain voiceless and powerless. Women are disproportionately affected by poverty, inequality and violence. It is widely estimated that women make up the majority of the world's poor, comprise nearly two thirds of the people who are illiterate, and, along with children, account for 80 per cent of civilian casualties during armed conflict.

All Member States of the United Nations, regardless of their political, religious or ethnic composition, spoke with one voice when the UN pledged to make the world fit for children at the General Assembly Special Session on Children in May 2002. But rallying around the cause of children without championing gender equality is like stocking a sports team with players but failing to teach them how to play the game.[43]

---

[43]   *The State of the World's Children*, 2007, 9–12

It is palpable that millions of women and girls have yet to be release from the dungeon of being voiceless and powerless. Discriminatory practices against females are still deeply ingrained in many societies. Those are societies where the demands for social reforms and gender equality have not been adequately met. Because of pervasive gender biases and mistreatments, millions of women now find themselves in a subordinated position in society and a sombre mood in their households. This should give us impetus to dedicate ourselves anew to the cause of their liberty.

Although the plights of women vary according to the geographical, economic, historical, and cultural circumstances, the amelioration and development of each should be accorded the same interest. Today's advanced knowledge should be applied to study and properly understand the telling problems which exist in the different countries of the world and, moreover, find the solutions to aid the victims in each to overcome their difficulties.

It saddens me, and no doubt others, to realise that the well-being and prospects of hundreds of millions of women and girls are still ravaged by sexist ideologies. Womanitarians must combine their efforts to adequately meet the needs and ease the problems of women and children. Helping deprived and vulnerable women and children is not over but only just beginning. It is vital to prolong efforts to extend all possible assistance in the improvement of women's lot. Surely, if we all render jointly our unsparing efforts to improve women's lives and reduce children's suffering, we would in a few short years achieve results far beyond what each of us, acting alone, could attain.

Violence and prejudicial actions can no longer be tolerable in a civilised world. Every human being has an inherent right to receive ethical treatment. The individual freedom and human dignity must be valued. Therefore, the inalienable rights of women and children must be respected. To assure this, it is vital to topple and destroy the last transgressions of feminism. Only this can assure that present and future generations of women may be born and live and die as equal to men. Deprivation and violations of the human rights of women can and must stop. This is the ultimatum presented to us whereby men must be persuaded to subordinate their immoral interests to the interests of humanity. These are the objectives, unobtainable yesterday, essential today, which we must strive to accomplish. Until this is achieved, women and girls will remain vulnerable to gender discrimination and disempowerment.

Chapter 47

Our Goal

Establishing true equality among humans should be of deep concern to all civilised people. Gender equality has become an urgent imperative of the world. This is not because it agitates for the elimination of sexism and chauvinism or because true equality will bring about the change in man's attitude requisite to the establishment of mutual love, respect, tolerance, peace, and amity between humans. To bring an end to all discriminatory practices is vital today because the principle of non-discrimination provides the springboard to help people forbid the vilification or disparagement of each other on the basis of one or more diverse characteristics such as gender, ethnicity, religion, race, etc. For certain, the democratic legislatures of civilised nations must preserve and promote the principles of liberty, equality, and individual freedom. The law must hard line against all incitements to violence and prejudicial actions.

Let us relish the challenge to make sure every human receive ethical treatment as their birthright. The human dignity of all individuals must be adequately safeguarded. In our opposition to human rights violations, we must take whatever measures required in obliterating from this world those disgraces to humanity and insults to women. It is a shame to our civilisation that the age-old ignorance of gender discrimination remains as problems affecting hundreds of millions of women and girls. This should urge us to labour without stint to assure that such reckless disregard for females may be eradicated during our lifetime. It will be a great day when all women are free from oppression and discrimination the world over. Surely, this should be considered our goal.

The goal of the equality of humans which we sought is the antithesis of subordination of one gender by the other. Throughout the world, a vigorous attack must be launched to eradicate the last vestiges of gender discrimination and disempowerment of women and girls. Gender discrimination is multifaceted. But whatever guise it assumes, this practice must be eliminated where it still exists. The dream of gender equality is long overdue to become reality to all women to whom it is still denied. This will in turn, give them courage and confidence to shrug off the amoralities which seek to oppress them. In order for women to achieve the true ideals of liberty and equality, a successful struggle must be waged against gender-based inequalities wherever it still exists. This struggle must also strive to guarantee that the practice is not reincarnated in other forms in areas whence it has already been discredited and abandoned.

Inaction is among the most pervasive violations of women's rights. Because of the condoning of gender inequalities on the part of those governments that failed thus far to accept fully CEDAW, it makes it so much more difficult for those who devoted to improving women's rights and living conditions to triumph. Societies that sow the seeds of gender equality, undoubtedly, will reap the reward of the double dividend. It is only proper for all governments to fully support the United Nations International Bill of Human Rights treaties and declarations such as the International Covenant on Economic, Social and Cultural Rights (ICESCR); Universal Declaration of Human Rights (UDHR); the International Covenant on Civil and Political Rights (ICCPR); the Convention on the Elimination of All Forms of Discrimination against Women; and the Convention on the Rights of the Child

(CRC). These international organs of rights, if implemented effectively, can end the vulnerability of women and children to violations of their rights. In our pursuit of women's rights, we most focus on appealing to the conscience of governments to fulfil their obligations to UN principles: 'economic development, social progress and human rights'.

It is not politic of civilised nations to tolerate the vulnerabilities of women and girls to human rights abuses. This only allows depraved men to prey upon them. As an example, domineering men continue to pattern themselves on intimate partner violence (IPV) against women. The violent script of Faith McNulty (1918–2005) in the non-fiction book *The Burning Bed* (1980, turned into a movie in 1984), about the spousal abuse against Francine Hughes (born August 1947), is replayed perpetually by abusive men against many housewives today. Wife-battering is very pervasive. It's palpable that feminist movements have only scratched the surface of the need to stop sexual abuse, emotional abuse, and economic deprivation against women and girls.

A great generation will not cease to try and improve on the past in order to meet newly arising demands to lessen the burden of its posterity. This is the path for us to follow. Characterised by the zeal of womanitarianism, we can endeavour to assure that the past and present injustices and inequalities are not repeated against women and girls in the future. Proponents of gender equality must, therefore, build on the success that our feminist forebears have bequeathed to us. We must endeavour to ensure the full advancement of women's human rights and fundamental freedoms on a basis of equality with men. Every female must gain equal rights and opportunities to achieve their full potential through creativity and independence.

Chapter 48

United Effort

To eliminate gender discrimination, that repugnant and loathsome practice, womanitarians and feminists must unite. It is not only the strength of male chauvinism and anti-feminism that delay success towards advancing complete women's rights but also the weakness of unity among those who have concern for or are involved with improving women's lives and reducing children's suffering. People can only achieve common goals through synergism. We must stand united to combat the misogynistic regime in order to prevail triumphant.

This battle will not be won easily. Great sacrifices will be required of us to assure victory. The united strength of morality is requisite to quell the last bastions of the misogynistic regime. Let us bring the combined pressure of womanitarianism and feminism to bear on anti-feminists and male chauvinists. Let us combine our efforts to repulse the stigma of gender discrimination from the earth. We must take up where our forebears have left off in transforming the equal academic, political, social, and economic status of humans. Humanity will only profit from the establishment of equality at all levels. For this would provide the mediums whereby humans sincerely tolerate each other. This will compel humans to respect the fact that they are actually interdependent and complement each other's weaknesses. We must do what is scrupulously required to transform our united aspirations into reality.

We must be mindful of the adage that 'united we stand divided we fall'. We must, therefore, be fully committed to unity to support and strengthen the cause for women's empowerment. Through such cooperation, we can expedite the social and economic progress of women. We know that unity can be and has been attained between people who share a common sense of purpose. With advanced technology of our time, physical distances are no insurmountable obstacles to the communication and coming together of peoples. The Internet now provides the transportation to link people together in the press of a button.

Challenging bias attitudes towards women also require a legislative and administrative approach. Governments should undertake legislative and financial measures to create a more just world for humans. Social policies should tackle discrimination at all levels of society. As womanitarians, we must redouble efforts to appeal to world leaders to implement CEDAW, CRC, and thus legislate against all discriminatory practices and customs.

Gender discriminations must become permanently abrogated. For until there is no longer gender-based favouritism of any level of society, women will continue to be vilified by male chauvinists as less important to men in more ways than one. For until the basic human rights are equally guaranteed to all members of the human family, the dream of gender equality will remain illusory. Until then, the male chauvinistic pigs will continue to hold women in subhuman bondage and enmesh them in a tangle with subservient roles. Without gender equality, women will simply remain disproportionately oppressed and subordinated.

All nations and people must join hands and pull together to fight the scourges of humanity. Both ordinary people and those who hold veto power must exert their efforts and wielded influences to promote gender equality and the empowerment of women and girls. It is the duty of the ordinary concerned individual to appeal to world leaders to tackle problems blighting the hopes of hundreds of millions of women and children. It is long overdue for all UN state parties to 'take all appropriate measures to ensure the full development and advancement of women so as to guarantee them the enjoyment of human rights and fundamental freedoms on a basis of equality with men. This is in all fields but in particular the political, social, economic and cultural fields,' as enshrined in Article 3 of CEDAW.

Unity of Organisations

There is a long history of organised endeavours to progress the liberty and human rights of the downtrodden masses of the world. There are many global human rights and feminist organisations. Members of these organisations, however, in their determination must cooperate and collaborate to achieve greater progress. It is only on this basis of unity, cooperation and goodwill the people who are dedicated to the struggle for elimination of all forms of discrimination and empowering women can achieve full success.

Because of the fundamental similarities and common factors between the various womanitarians involved with improving women's lives and reducing children suffering, they must adopt the principle of synergism for the establishment of greater cooperation, which will be for their mutual benefit. These organisations all have a cause in common to promote the warfare of women and children and to protect them against human rights abuses. But if all these organisations do not combine their weight, then their individual pressure will never be enough to end violence and discrimination against women and girls. This is precisely why the non-governmental organisations (NGO) should collaborate with each other so that the pressure now applies on societies to eliminate gender discrimination will be augmented. International womanitarian cooperation will definitely quicken the pace for progress of universal equality. The individual organisations do not carry the weight to do this.

Only full cooperation and synergism among all democracy organisations can bring success to the endeavours for the interest and benefit for all people. Despite their size, the individual organisations are weak. There are estimated millions of NGOs pursuing social, political, and economic aims. India, for example, is estimated to have had around 3.3 million NGOs in 2009. Also, NGOs in the United States are estimated at 1.5 million. However, whatever these organisations have achieved individually cannot be considered sufficient in their area of advocacy. This is exactly why they are still in operation, struggling for the same cause for decades. Through the process of assimilation and amalgamation, these organisations can establish the strength to achieve their common interests to ameliorate poverty, expand education, health care, and women's rights. Unity of strength and purpose are indispensable to raise the global standard of living for the benefit of humanity. Without unity, it is impossible to achieve progress, peace, harmony, and equality.

Chapter 49

Stand Up for Gender Equality

Eliminating gender discrimination and empowering women are among the urgent imperatives facing our world today. I say this not only because it equates women with men, or because I believe it will bring an end to gender-based inequalities, or because the elimination of gender discrimination will bring in its wake those changes in attitudes and customs so requisite to the espousal of feminism. I say this simply because discrimination, in all its forms, is an additional impediment to the moral and intellectual progress of humans. Without the total eradication of de facto discrimination, it is impossible to constitute total neighbourliness and equity among people. The acceleration of de jure equality will ensure further advancement of the human rights and fundamental freedom of women equal with men.

Impartiality of the justice system and unbiased opinion of the individuals are, undoubtedly, key to society's progress in ethical, humane, and reasonable practices. Above all, society must avoid the pitfalls of institutional discrimination. This only opens the doors to sexism, classism, and racism to creep in with harmful consequences. These ideologies only corrupt the minds of people of low morals. This inevitably destroys the foundation for peace, harmony, and oneness among people.

We must realize that inequality is an obstacle to be overcome in order to create a brighter future and happier life for women and children. Equality is indispensible to women's empowerment and human progress.

Gender equality is central to realizing the Millennium agenda, which risks failure without the full participation of all members of society. Within the Millennium Declaration and the Millennium Development Goals, and at the heart of the United Nations itself, is the acknowledgement that the vulnerable, especially children, require special care and attention. Gender equality will not only empower women to overcome poverty, but also their children, families, communities and countries. When seen in this light, gender equality is not only morally right— it is pivotal to human progress and sustainable development.

Moreover, gender equality produces a double dividend: It benefits both women and children. Healthy, educated and empowered women have healthy, educated and confident daughters and sons. The amount of influence women have over the decisions in the household has been shown to positively impact the nutrition, health care and education of their children. But the benefits of gender equality go beyond their direct impact on children. Without it, it will be impossible to create a world of equity, tolerance and shared responsibility—a world that is fit for children.

Yet, despite substantial gains in women's empowerment since the Convention on the Elimination of All Forms of Discrimination

against Women was adopted by the UN General
Assembly in 1979, gender discrimination remains
pervasive in every region of the world. It appears
in the preference for sons over daughters, limited
opportunities in education and work for girls and
women, and outright gender-based violence in the
forms of physical and sexual violence.

Other, less obvious, forms of gender discrimination
can be equally destructive. Institutional
discrimination is harder to identify and rectify.
Cultural traditions can perpetuate social exclusion
and discrimination from generation to generation,
as gender stereotypes remain widely accepted and
go unchallenged.

Eliminating gender discrimination and
empowering women will require enhancing
women's influence in the key decisions that shape
their lives and those of children in three distinct
arenas: the household, the workplace and the
political sphere. A change for the better in any one
of these realms influences women's equality in the
others and has a profound and positive impact on
children everywhere.[44]

Women's rights, although legislated, is not yet total—areas of
resistance still remain. These are issues we must militate against
for the final liberation of those women still dominated by male
chauvinistic pigs. Human rights are meaningless unless all
members of the human family are free to exercise their inherent
dignity and inalienable rights. Liberty must be equally guaranteed
to all humans as their birthright. As a result of the all-pervasive

---

[44]   *The State of the World's Children*, 2007, viii

violations of women's rights, hundreds of millions of our sisters of the human family in the Americas, in Asia, in Europe, in Africa, and in Oceania yowl in anguish for our help. To assure that their pleas don't go unheeded, we must align and identify ourselves with all aspects of their struggle. The UN member states for their part have pledged to assess progress in fulfilling the MDGs. But it is a moral crime of anyone who pays only lip service to the cause of improving women's lives and reducing children's suffering. Therefore, we must back our words with meaningful action to promote the advancement of women's welfare. Don't belittle yourself, stand up for your belief in equality—your support is highly valuable to global advancement of equity and social justice.

Chapter 50

Final Call for Gender Equality

I t is evident that bias gesture and conduct that vilifies women as inferior is an incitement to violence and prejudicial action against them. It is poignant that millions of women live a very subordinate and unhappy life in the twenty-first century, as there are men, in their arrogance and ignorance, continue to discriminate against women, judging them on the basis of gender rather than by their intelligence and abilities. This practice remains as a problem affecting the human rights and fundamental freedoms of women in the political, economic, social, cultural, and civil spheres of society the world over.

Adequate and effective protection of women and girls against all acts of discrimination can and must be achieved. Gender discrimination is an insult to women. It casts a heavy burden upon them. Educating boys to refrain from engaging in acts of discrimination against women and girls is a pivotal step towards the elimination of the practice. As exponents of equality, we must teach our sons and nephews to abhor all forms of discrimination. If the young men of present generation are not taught the principle of the equality of men and women, the cycle of social and economic equalities will spin on. In the upbringing and development of children, parents must refrain from practising stereotype roles for boys and girls. Parents must be careful not to show favouritism towards any one of their children. This will help to eliminate chauvinistic ideology of the inferiority and the superiority of the sexes. Breaking the patterns of stereotypes and prejudice against women and girls should begin at home. Teach the youths to say *no* to violence and discrimination against women and girls.

To accelerate progress towards a better and a more just world, children must learn to heap scorn on violence and prejudicial actions against each other on the basis of disability, ethnicity, gender, nationality, religion, race, etc. Since moral responsibilities will be entrusted tomorrow to the children of today, all appropriate measures must be taken to ensure they develop the most unimpeachable integrity and character. This will help to bring to fruition our hopes and aspirations for a brighter and happier future for coming generations. In view to eliminate discrimination against women and girls, greater emphasis must be placed on teaching boys to understand the values of being chivalrous towards females. It is fitting to teach them that women are not, by any means, naturally less important, intelligent, or able than men.

The conducts and views of parental figures generally influence children during their formative years. Girls tend to replicate their mothers' habits, whether positive or negative, while boys tend to replicate those of their father figures. Parental figures that have positive relationships will augment the chance of their children developing positive regard of themselves and others. For equity and social justice, society must condemn hate speech, inequality, intolerance, and bigotry. Amoral acts cannot justify moral means. Children must be well disciplined to avoid the pejorative words of ethnic, religious, and sexist slurs. Indiscipline and misguided children are prone to disturb the peace of society with antisocial behaviour and maladjustment. Disrespectful behaviour and contemptuous manners are useless to peaceful coexistence. It is also useless to pay lip service to the cause for eliminating discrimination and advancing the full implementation of the international bill of rights for women and children. All those who have the best interests of women and children at heart, no doubt, must be fully devoted to their betterment.

Equality must be implemented adequately in order for present and future generations to enjoy the latent good of the international instruments of human rights.

> For children to achieve their fullest potential and to grow up in families and societies where they can thrive, gender discrimination must be banished once and for all. A world free of discrimination may seem like an impossible dream, but it is a dream within our reach. In recent decades, the goal of reducing gender discrimination has steadily grown in importance on the international agenda. Corresponding successes in empowering women and girls have become increasingly apparent. Since 1945, the proportion of women in parliament has increased more than fivefold. Girls' education has increased dramatically in many regions . . . Discriminatory attitudes towards women and girls have been changing.

Progress is reflected in statistical outcomes and in the underlying social and political processes that have resulted in a strong international consensus in support of gender equality and the rights of girls and women . . . But despite these gains and commitments, for many women, adolescent girls and girl children, the promises have not materialized. From children excluded from education because of their gender, to adolescent girls who may die from problems related to pregnancy and childbirth or face violence and sexual abuse, gender discrimination leads to rights violations that reverberate throughout the life cycle.[45] (See Chapter 22 *Cycle of Gender Discrimination*)

---

[45]   *The State of the World's Children*, 2007, 69

Self-evidently, it is a challenge of great complexity to liberate those women and girls who're still experiencing upheaval by discriminatory practices. On behalf of those deprived and vulnerable women and girls, let us struggle unstintingly for their liberation. Eliminating prejudices and stereotypes of gender roles will make a real difference in the lives of millions of women and girls. It would be betrayal were we to lose focus on what must be done to achieve gender equality and women's empowerment. And to do this, we must act now. The answers to the problems affecting women and children are, in fact, efficient and adequate actions.

Glossary

Foremother (*fawr-muh*th-*er*) noun: a female ancestor or a woman who lived in the past.

Womanitarian (*woo-maen-i-tair-ee-an*) adjective/noun: (1) a person who has concern for or is involved with improving women's lives and reducing children's suffering. (2) One who has the interests of womankind at heart and is devoted to promote the advancement of women's welfare.

Womanitarianism (woo-*maen-i-tair-ee-a-ni-zem*) noun: (1) the doctrine that humanity's obligations are concerned wholly with the welfare of womankind. (2) Womanitarian principles or practices.